Introduction to Using the Psion Series 3

by Rod Lawton & Isaac Davis

ISBN 07457 0146 9

CW00762275

Published by:

Kuma Computers Ltd
12 Horseshoe Park
Pangbourne
Berks
RG8 7JW

Tel 0734 844335
Fax 0734 844339

Introduction to Using the Psion Series 3

©1992 Rod Lawton & Isaac Davis

Other Computing Titles From Kuma:

IBM PC & Compatible Micros

DTP Sourcebook - Fonts & Clip Art for the PC by J. L. Borman	07457 0030 6
PageMaker 4.0 for Windows by William B. Sanders	07457 0031 4
ZBasic Quick Reference Guide for PC & Mac by John Sumner	07457 0140 X
The Windows Guide Book by Gill Gerhardi, Vic Gerhardi & Andy Berry	07457 0041 1
A Practical Guide to Timeworks Publisher 2 on the PC by Terry Freedman	07457 0147 7
The DR DOS 6 Quick Start Guide by John Sumner	07457 0038 1
Illustrated DR DOS 6 - The First 20 Hours by John Sumner	07457 0044 6
The User's Guide to Money Manager PC by John Sumner	07457 0047 0
Breaking Into Windows 3.1 by Bill Stott & Mark Brearley	07457 0056 X
The Utter Novice Guide to GW Basic by Bill Aitken	07457 0045 4
The Utter Novice Guide to Q Basic by Bill Aitken	07457 0046 2
PagePlus Illustrated by Richard Hunt	07457 0062 4
DOS 5 Quick Start Guide by John Sumner	07457 0054 3

Commodore Amiga

Program Design Techniques for the Amiga by Paul Overaa	07457 0032 2
Intuition A Practical Programmers Guide by Mike Nelson	07457 0143 4
The Little Red Workbench 1.3 Book by Mark Smiddy	07457 0048 9
The Little Blue Workbench 2 Book by Mark Smiddy	07457 0055 1

Apple Macintosh

DTP Sourcebook - Fonts & Clip Art for the Mac by J. L. Borman	07457 0050 0
ZBasic Quick Reference Guide for PC & Mac by John Sumner	07457 0140 X
The Quark Book by Rod Lawton & Isaac Davis	07457 0052 7

Psion Organiser

Psion Organiser Deciphered by Gill Gerhardi, Vic Gerhardi & Andy Berry	07457 0139 6
Using & Programming the Psion Organiser by Mike Shaw	07457 0134 5
File Handling on the Psion Organiser by Mike Shaw	07457 0135 3
Machine Code Programming on the Psion Organiser 2nd Ed. by Bill Aitken	07457 0138 8
Psion Organiser Comms Handbook by Gill & Vic Gerhardi & Andy Berry	07457 0154 X

Psion Series 3

First Steps in Programming the Psion Series 3 by Mike Shaw	07457 0145 0
Serious Programming on the Psion Series 3 by Bill Aitken	07457 0035 7

Atari ST

Atari ST Explored 2nd Ed. by John Braga & Malcolm McMahon	07457 0141 8
Program Design Techniques for the Atari ST by Paul Overaa	07457 0029 2
Programming by Example - ST Basic by Dr. G. McMaster	07457 0142 6
A Practical Guide to Calamus Desktop Publishing by Terry Freedman	07457 0159 0
A Practical Guide to Timeworks on the Atari ST by Terry Freedman	07457 0158 2

Cambridge Z88

Z88 Magic by Gill Gerhardi, Vic Gerhardi & Andy Berry	07457 0137 X

Games

Sega Megadrive Secrets by Rusel deMaria	07457 0037 3
Sega Megadrive Secrets Volume 2 by Rusel deMaria	07457 0043 8
Corish's Computer Games Guide	07457 0150 7
Awesome Sega Megadrive Secrets	07457 0226 0

Sharp IQ 7000 & 8000

Using Basic on the Sharp IQ by John Sumner	07457 0034 9

A selection from our fast-expanding range - latest full details on request

CONTENTS

HOW TO USE THIS BOOK

We've written this book knowing that we'll be catering for a variety of readers. Some people will want specific information about their Series 3 straight away. Some will want explanations of the machine's principal features. Some will just want to know where to start!

• **We're assuming that you've already unpacked your Series 3 and got it up and running – i.e. the batteries are inserted & the correct time is set. If not, get to it! Follow the instructions in the User Guide.**

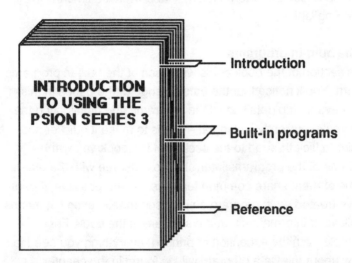

This book has been organised into three sections so as to be accessible to users at all levels

The book consists of three distinct sections, comprising a general introduction, using the applications and reference:

I Introduction to computing and the Series 3
This section tells you what to do with the Series 3 when you get

1

it out of the box, how to set it up, how the various programs work and interrelate, which keys do what and so on.

We also explain how you use the programs – what are menus and dialogs? What does 'selecting an option' mean? The Series 3's programs are designed to be easy and quick to use, but first of all you have to know what's what.

There's a great deal of jargon in computing (do we need to tell you that?) and we explain it simply. Not everyone is 'computer-literate' and not everyone has the time to study the arcane jargon so beloved of computer owners. For those of you still struggling with the gobbledygook, there's a special chapter devoted to computer terminology – and what it all means in plain English!

II The built-in programs

This section of the book deals with each of the built-in programs in turn. You'll notice that the outside edge of the pages in this part have a strip detailing all the programs and highlighting the one you're currently looking at – this is to make it quicker and easier to flick through to the section of the book you want.

Some of the programs interrelate to a degree with the others. Some of them share common features. Where possible, though, we've treated each program entirely separately, even if it means duplicating information found elsewhere in the book. For example, with the exception of printing, everything you need to know about the Data program will be found in the chapter devoted to it – none of this 'see page x, y, z' nonsense! (At least, where it's humanly possible to avoid it.)

III Reference

The reference section at the back of the book contains information on printing, transfer of files to other machines, data security, plugging-in the various Psion peripherals available and troubleshooting. See this section for topics relating to the machine itself rather than any specific program.

Just beginning?

Some of the people reading this book will never have used a computer before. Others will know the things inside out. Bear with us! We begin each chapter assuming no prior computing knowledge on the part of the reader. Then, as we progress to more advanced topics within the chapter, we assume that you're trying out the examples and picking up the jargon. By the end of the chapter we've covered all the features the program offers and introduced all the necessary terms and phrases.

However, you don't have to finish each chapter to start using the machine. When you've found out what you currently want – or need – to know, why not stop there? You can come back to the chapter later when you need a bit more information or you've had time to assimilate what you've already read. This book is a work of reference, not a work of art – read what you need! And have fun with your new toy...

INTRODUCTION

It all started with the Filofax. This has become the symbol of yuppies everywhere – which is a shame, since the ordinary personal organiser is an incredibly useful item for any business executive – or any busy mother, for that matter.

The idea is that your personal organiser should be a repository for all the information you need in your day-to-day activities. The organiser, a miniature loose-leaf filing system, is divided up into sections, according to function. Need a telephone number? Look it up in the 'phone book section. Making a date for dinner? Put it in the diary section. Drawing up a list of possible birthday presents for your spouse? There's a section for jotting down notes, too.

But personal organisers aren't perfect. Whenever you change a piece of information you have to cross out the old one. Paper is fragile, and frequently-thumbed pages soon become dog-eared, and can even fall out. And as you put in more and more information your pocket filing system soon gets filled to bursting point, which is where the electronic organiser comes in.

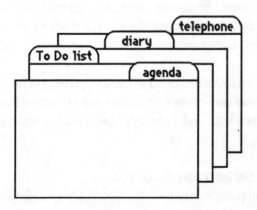

Electronic and traditional paper-based organisers work

using the same principles. Information is split up into separate compartments – like a miniature filing cabinet.

Computers are excellent devices for handling information. They can store vast quantities of the stuff and retrieve it rapidly. Information can be edited and deleted at will and – best of all – electronic organisers are small enough to slip into pockets which would never take the traditional, paper-based equivalent.

But what's this? – we've mentioned the word 'computer'. At the same time as people everywhere were discovering the delights of personal organisers, they were also discovering that computers could revolutionise their work. In particular, the preparation of reports, the storing of client lists... even the drafting of novels.

And people also began to realise that a *portable* computer – like a portable typewriter, only more so – could be more useful still. Hence the quest for ever smaller and lighter portable computers...

...Culminating in a genuinely pocket-sized machine like the Psion Series 3.

That's right – the Psion is as much a computer as it is a simple electronic 'organiser'. While lacking the power and versatility of a desktop machine, it can still act as an excellent 'companion', letting you carry out office work while away from the office.

Is the wee beast too good to be true? Well, the Series 3 does have its flaws and limitations, but it's still just about the most versatile, powerful and genuinely useful pocket computer to date.

What the Series 3 can do for you
Pocket computer it may be – the Series 3's greatest strength is nevertheless it's ability to do just what it says – 'organise'. What can it do for *you*?

Notes

The Series 3 features a standard typewriter QWERTY key layout, and as such is great news for writers everywhere! Many pocket organisers feature an alphabetic layout, which is OK for those not used to using keyboards, or if you only want to write short notes for yourself, but it's a nightmare for longer pieces, since it takes as long to find the letters you want as it does to type out the words.

The Series 3's QWERTY layout, on the other hand, is fast and easy to use. And the built-in word processing software is in many ways as powerful as that found on desktop computers. The Series 3's keyboard is too small for touch-typing, but it still allows very rapid text entry, making the machine ideal for writing while on the move. Even more so since it can be used standing up - one hand holding the machine, the other typing. (BR commuters who spend hours waiting on platforms take note!)

Reports and articles

The Series 3 is capable of more than simple note-taking, however. Unlike most electronic pocket organisers, it features extremely powerful and versatile word-processing software. Sophisticated 'outlining' features let you plan major pieces of work easily, and the machine has more than enough storage capacity for long documents. Indeed, its features would put to shame those on many a proper word-processing program on a desktop machine. This is helped by very comprehensive printing facilities – with the appropriate cable the Series 3 can send its output directly to most popular printers.

Letters

The Series 3 is also handy when opening your correspondence - the word processor can be used for formulating your replies, while the database software will store all the names and addresses you need.

Telephone calls

Do you spend a lot of time on the telephone? If so, the advantages of being able to recall hundreds of telephone numbers with just a few keypresses are obvious. But the Psion does more than that – if you have a tone-dialling telephone, it will even dial those numbers for you!

Not only that, it can work out the international dialling codes for any country in the world *from* any country. Now all you have to worry about is the time difference... except that the Series 3 can tell you that too!

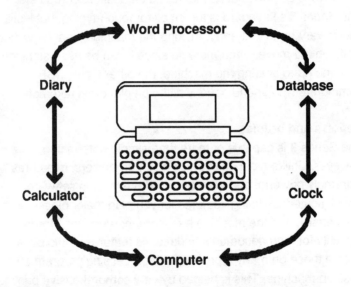

The Series 3 offers not just several different 'organiser' functions, it links them together so that they can work interdependently.

Calculations

The Series 3 can also double as a simple pocket calculator - it's not a great deal larger than one. Apart from all the standard arithmetic functions, however, the machine will also allow a range of complex scientific functions. There are ten calculator memories available, and numbers can be displayed in exponential format and to the number of decimal places you specify (if you want to display answers to two decimal places, say, the Series 3 will still calculate to 12 decimal places, but will round the answer up or down).

Appointments

Is your diary a dog-eared, bulging mess of scratched-out entries, odd bits of paper with notes scribbled on them and old business cards? The Series 3 is purpose-built to put that right. The joy of an electronic organiser is that you can clean it out and retain only that information you need. You can also retrieve that information in seconds using sophisticated 'find' functions that will make the bad old days of thumbing desperately through disintegrating notebooks a thing of the past. What are you doing the day after tomorrow at 3pm? How about six months time? A year? With the Series 3, storing information like this is easy, and retrieving it later easier still. You can even remind yourself about forthcoming appointments via alarms!

To Do lists

If you're a busy executive, the chances are you keep a To Do list – a list of jobs you have to get done. You might well assign 'priorities' to these jobs. The Series 3 has software to do just this as part of its Agenda program. You can also store notes for specific days as well as a general list of things 'to do'.

Data storage

Personal organisers are handy things to have… at first. The trouble is, before long they begin bursting at the seams. Oft-used pages start to drop out as the binder holes tear; more items are crossed out than are filled in as you update your information; precious moments are spent scrabbling through the pages as you desperately seek information required by a superior or a caller... the Psion Series 3 makes all this a thing of the past with database software that lets you store wide varieties of information and retrieve it in seconds.

Names and addresses, company listings, inventories, even birdwatching notes... you can store any information you like, in whatever form you like.

A helping hand...
The Series 3 may be a godsend to anyone with more jobs and information to handle than they have time to handle it in, but you can't just pick it up and use it straight away. Although it's designed to be as simple and intuitive to use as possible, some of its features are quite complex. Actually, some of them are downright obscure. Similarly, some of its functions are more useful than others...

You could sit down and plod your way through all the options systematically. For this we suggest you give up your job, make sure your family is provided for and then go and live in a cave in the Andes.

Alternatively, read on...

COMPUTER TERMINOLOGY

It sometimes seems like the computer is an impenetrable affair impossible to understand when you're a computer novice. Bits, bytes, ROMs and RAM – an avalanche of jargon all designed to keep the uninitiated firmly out of the picture.

Well, that's what it *seems* like, sure, but in fact, the nomenclature is no more difficult to understand than when you learned the jargon associated with stamp collecting or fishing. The necessary understanding seemed impossible to achieve, but all too soon, you were performing like a professional.

Remember too, even the professionals started out wondering what in Heaven's name ROM and RAM was...

So let's penetrate that dusty silicon veil and discover just what lies beneath.

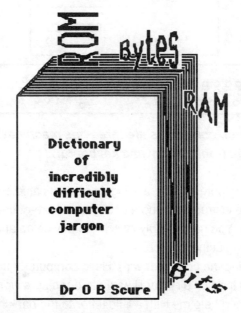

Dictionary of incredibly difficult computer jargon

Dr O B Scure

Beat the jargon by reading this chapter!

Lifting the lid...

The computer consists of a series of building blocks each with a distinct function, and each working closely with the others to provide what you see as an end-user: an electronic computer able to process data meaningfully.

Even the most hardened techno-phobe has *seen* a computer, and that means you're already familiar with two of the building blocks, namely, the keyboard and the display screen.

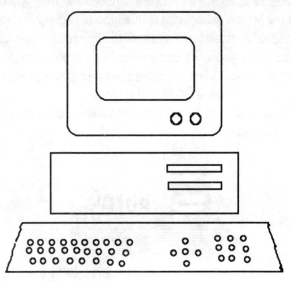

Most desktop computers are three-box machines: screen display, electronic 'brain' and keyboard...

Although computers today are highly sophisticated beasts, they must still be instructed using a sequence of pre-defined commands. You can't simply switch the device on and tell it to do something using speech.

Addressing the computer with "Hello computer. I hope you're feeling well today. I'd rather like you to open up a word processor and help me with a little letter to the bank manager..." will get you nothing more than the silicon equivalent of a blank stare. Instead, you have to *type* the relevant and pre-defined commands into the machine, in way in which it can understand.

• **Computers are instructed using precise, pre-defined command sequences.**

The above may go something like this when translated into computer-speil:

DIR <return key>
RUN TYPEZEE <return key>

The first *command*, DIR, tells the computer to display all the programs it has stored within it (don't worry, we'll explain programs and storage in a moment…). The second command tells the machine to run – that is, open up and enable you to use a word processor called TYPEZEE.

Notice how the return key has to be pressed each time a command is typed into the system. The return key is similar to that on an ordinary typewriter, but unlike it's mechanical counterpart, rather than *return*ing the carriage, the computer's return key tells the machine that we've type in an instruction and would now like to have it *processed*.

This type of interface between the user and the computer is known as a 'command line interface' or CLI for short. It was used extensively on the first personal computers such as those from IBM (you may have encountered one or two at work or college). It's called an interface by the way, because it acts as a middle-man, accepting your instructions and passing them on to the computer's inner workings.

In an attempt to make things easier for the non-computer literate, computer manufacturers came up with the idea of providing a pictorial interface between the computer and the user. That is, instead of you having to type in each command to look at what's stored inside the machine, or run a program, the program provides little pictures ('icons') representing storage, programs and so on on. If you want to look at what's stored or run an application (another name for a program) then you select the picture and press return. Thus there's no need to remember often-obscure commands.

Just like the command line interface or CLI, the pictorial interface also has a short-hand name. It's called a GUI or Graphical User Interface (the graphics in this instance being the little pictures or *icons* that are displayed for you to select).

So that's the keyboard building block. It's there to enable you to input instructions.

See how during the course of the keyboard description (a device you're already familiar with and so comfortable discussing...) you've learned a lot of the nomenclature already? Icons, CLI, GUI, interface, all on board. Painless, right?

GUIs feature tiny pictures known as 'icons' which represent computer applications. Icons are selected by moving an arrow (the 'pointer') over them and clicking with a mouse, or pressing a designated key on the keyboard

The other main block of the computer which is visible to the outside world is its display screen or *monitor*. Just as the computer cannot accept verbal instructions from you, it is also dumb – no speech will ever issue forth from electronic lips.

Instead, a display screen is provided for the poor machine to inform you of pertinent happenings. The results of some calculations perhaps, or the fact that it's running short of memory or power.

Many desktop computers have large monitors attached which look rather like domestic television sets. Fine. But for owners of the Psion Series 3, lugging a portable TV around to act as a display would pretty much defeat the point of having a palm-top computer. After all, it's useful precisely because it can be slipped into a pocket.

So to get around that particular hurdle, the machine is equipped with a built-in LCD screen. This display acts exactly like the monsters atop the average desk-bound computer, but it's small, lightweight, built into the machine's case and – most importantly – being LCD, it requires very little power.

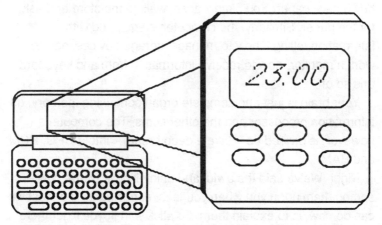

Just like your watch, the Series 3 uses an LCD screen to output information. LCD technology uses little power and is – literally – crystal clear!

OK. We have a keyboard to get instructions into the computer, and a monitor to receive the processed results of the instructions back. But what's going on inside? What happens when the return key is pressed and instructions entered? How is information displayed on the monitor?

Brain the size of a planet!

At the very centre of every computer is an electronic brain which is remarkable similar to yours. Just like the grey jelly splurging about in your head, this electronic brain can memorise information, process it, and output it in a sensible way (at least, we *hope* yours can…). And just like your brain, the computer's has a series of 'instructions' which it never forgets and which are always available when it 'wakes up' (or when the power is applied).

For you, these always-available instructions consist of information on how to breath, how to walk, how to talk – you don't have to re-learn that information every time you want to go buy a newspaper. You simply arise, walk to the store and ask for the paper. Similarly, the computer is equipped with information telling it how to manage storage devices, how to work a monitor, how to receive information from and keyboard and so on.

Your brain is just one complete organ containing memory, an information processor and the other items. The computer's however, is divided up – take a deep breath – into a CPU, ROM and RAM.

Right. We've said the awful and unintelligible words now – sprang them upon you when you least expected it. The least we can do now, is to explain them. So stick with it, you'll get there, OK?

The CPU or Central *Processing* Unit (sometimes called MPU Micro Processing Unit, or simply Processor), is the processing part of the computer's brain. The CPU accepts instructions in a form it can readily understand, processes them and outputs the results. Simple as that! No fuss, no lumps of fat or gristle, just straightforward processing, exactly like your brain, or a pocket

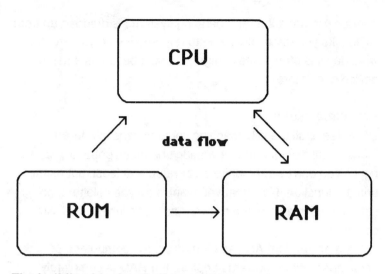

The building blocks of all computers...

calculator – even an abacus (although the CPU is automatic, the abacus has to be operated manually). The concept is the same. Information processing.

To do the processing, the CPU needs instructions. Some long-term instructions telling it how to manipulate keyboards, monitors and so on on (like your's telling you how to walk and talk...), and it also needs some short-term instructions telling it what a word processor is or what a space invader game is supposed to do.

The long-term memory is the ROM (Read Only Memory). This contains all the information the computer needs to behave as a responsible machine in a harsh world. Monitors, keyboards, printers, how to do mathematics - it's all there. You can't put any more information into the ROM because what's there already is all the computer needs to know how to operate. Hence the name *Read Only* Memory – you can read what's there, but not *write* to it (read and write mean 'take' and 'put' in silicon-speil). When the machine is switched on, the necessary

17

operating information (or 'operating system') is dredged up from ROM (like you frantically trying to remember who you are and what day it is after a heavy night…) and it becomes a useful device once more.

Ever more useful

Of course, if all the silly machine could do was to operate monitors all day long then it wouldn't be much good to you, right? You don't want monitors operated – at least, not as the primary function. No! What you want is to type in letters, do calculations, play a game or two. And that's where the RAM comes in.

RAM or Random Access Memory, is the computer's scratchpad. When power is applied, the RAM is completely empty. You decide what goes into this short-term memory and consequently, what the computer actually *does*. Run a game i.e. issue the command which gets the game from *backing* storage (more in a moment) and loads it into the RAM memory, and the computer becomes a games-playing machine. Run a spreadsheet and it becomes an actuary, performing calculations at the drop of a hat.

In our body analogy, the RAM is similar to your short-term memory. Thirty minutes first thing in the morning might be given over to jogging, but then things get serious. You go to work and total figures all day long. In the evenings a game of golf or a beverage or two at the local hostelry might be in order. From the moment of awakening, your brain knows that it should tell you to behave like a human being (ROM), but you decide what should happen thereafter (RAM).

Just like you, the computer is a multi-purpose device able to perform lots of actions depending upon its instructions. ROM ensures that it always behaves like a computer, never trying to act like a dog or a monkey, but RAM gives the device the opportunity or doing just whatever *you* want it to.

Backing up

There is a third type of memory known as backing storage. ROM, remember, contains a finite amount of instructions - just enough to get the computer to operate correctly, but no more. If the computer is do to something worthwhile, then you need to load instructions into the short-term RAM memory. But where do these instructions come from?

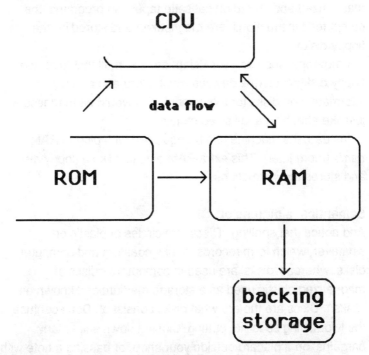

Short-term memory is only useful if you can store and retrieve it when it's needed – that's where backing storage comes in

The instructions for a word processor, for example, might be thousands of lines long. Do you have to type these into the machine each time you want it to behave like a word processor? Well, as we're sure you already know, the answer is a fortunate no! If they had to be typed in, you'd soon get sick of using what is supposed to be a time-saving device.

Instead the instructions are stored in a third form of memory known as 'backing storage'. Usually, floppy and hard disks. These are disc versions of the magnetic tape used in domestic cassettes. A form of plastic, coated with an iron-oxide substance able to be magnetized. In the way music is magnetized and stored on cassette tapes, so programs, the computer's instructions, are magnetized and stored on the floppy disks.

Palm-tops, such as your Psion, are so small that to attach floppy disk drives (the devices which store and retrieve information on disks for the computer...) would be madness – just like attaching a full sized monitor.

Instead, the machine can be equipped with plug-in RAM *cards* (more later). This extra RAM acts just like a floppy disk and stores the instructions.

Semantics: a digression
And notice that spelling. 'Dis*cs*' are circles of plastic or whatever, which form records, drinks coasters and computer disks, whereas 'dis*ks*' are used in computers - discs of magnetized plastic used as a storage medium and known as 'disks'). Discs are the are what disks consist of. Don't confuse the two. Doing so is like putting 'Closing down sail - many bargains' on a placard outside your shop, or passing a note with 'Please hoist the main sale...' to the Captain of a ship. They may sound the same, but they're *not* interchangeable, and you'd be surprised at the number of people, including those who ought to know better, who get it wrong!

Here endeth the first lesson
And that, you'll be relieved to hear, is the end of your first lesson in computer hardware – the electronic components which make

up the machine. A keyboard to enter instructions, and a monitor to read off the results. A CPU to process the instructions, ROM to hold the operating system so that the poor computer knows how to operate when it's awakened with electricity, short-term memory called RAM to store our instructions and get the machine to do something useful, and backing storage, so that we don't have to keep typing the instructions in every time we want to use them. Keyboard, monitor, CPU, ROM and RAM, and the floppy disks, the building blocks of every computer.

Soft options

So that's the hardware, but what's this *soft*ware you've heard so much about? Relax. With your new-found knowledge, learning about software is going to be very easy.

Remember those instructions held on backing storage? The ones which get the otherwise stupid computer to perform some useful task?

That's software.

Programs, applications, packages. Call them what you will, they're the lists of instructions which get the computer to perform for us. See, we humans are not impressed with monitor manipulation. The fact that the dumb beast can manage a keyboard is neither here nor there. What *we* want is labour-saving help, otherwise, it's off with the electricity and goodbye cruel world for the computer. Software *is* that labour-saving help.

There's also another form of information held on disks, and it's known as *data*. Think of it this way. You're using a typewriter. Just an ordinary, everyday, mechanical typewriter to produce a letter to your bank manager. The typewriter itself is the hardware, the paper within it the backing storage, and the software is your knowledge of how to operate a typewriter - the instructions in your head which keep your fingertips tapping down the keys at sixty words per minute. But what's that stuff *on* the paper? The information the software has produced and the backing storage is holding? Well, that's the *data*. Useful information, generated by you, processed and stored.

To return to the computer then, the machine itself is the hardware. Word processor instructions, the software, and the floppy disk is the backing storage medium upon which it's all held. And the letters, words and sentences are the data. Similarly, the calculations and equations generated and manipulated by your spreadsheet software are also data. Names and address in a database? More data.

Obviously, this data has to be safely stored. Just like the software, it's no good if it has to be typed in every time. So data is stored on disk in the form of *files*. Little pockets or nodules of information pertinent to a particular program and relevant to you and your needs.

So the computer and it's various attachments form the hardware, and the programs or *applications* stored on disk the software. The information which you manipulate using these two 'wares' are the data files. Look at any disk and you'll see applications and data waiting to work together to solve your problems.

The little extras...
The building blocks explained above provide a working computer system. Data in, bit of processing, and useful information out. But like all machines, a few go-faster stripes can sometimes ease or simplify the process. Think of it this way. A Reliant Robin will get you from A to B, but turbo charge the engine and uprate the brakes to match, and you'll do the journey just that little bit faster!

And the situation is the same silicon-wise. Early personal computers had poor keyboards, domestic cassette tape as backing storage, and family televisions as displays. Today, you get a much better system for your money ('system', by the way, is a word used to describe not just the computer, but its backing storage, display screen and anything else which may be attached), but the machines still benefit from add-on devices designed to uprate or ease the process of computing.

Many machines can have a hard disk drive added (a kind of very fast floppy disk), printers attached and more – if there's even a vague need for it, someone, somewhere will have cobbled one together and attempted to relieve you of hard cash for it.

Also in the early days of small computing, RAM was incredibly expensive. Most machines came equipped with a just a couple of K ('kilobyte', a measure of RAM). Compare that with the 256K installed in a machine which can sit in your hand!

The ideal for backing storage has always been to use RAM. If your instructions are always held close to the computer's brain, then the machine will be much faster to use. But prohibitive RAM costs meant that only a small amount of RAM could be installed, enough to take say, one program and its associated data, and the rest had to be held on backing storage.

Nowadays, RAM is much cheaper (and much smaller too!), and it's perfectly possible for machines such as the Psion to use RAM 'cards' as a backing storage medium. These cards are plastic-encased slivers of RAM which plug into slots at the side of the machine. This means that as well as the fairly large built-in 256K RAM which can hold lots of programs and data files, more RAM can be plugged in whenever it's needed.

There are a range of RAM cards available in various sizes for your machine. You probably won't need them at first, but as your knowledge and use of the Psion Series 3 grows, so will your needs. Soon, you'll have a little family of RAM cards all of your own!

MENUS, DIALOGS AND POINTERS

Gone – thankfully – are the days when you had to type in every command that a computer was expected to carry out. And woe betide you if you should get so much as a letter, never mind a word, wrong! These days computers are much more 'friendly'. And one of the ways in which they've become more friendly is the incorporation of the 'menu'

A menu is simply a list of commands or options available to you at any one time. These options tend to be grouped together according to their purpose, so that all options connected with handling documents, for example, would be grouped together on one menu, e.g. Open File, Close File, New File and Delete File would be found on a program's 'File' menu.

'Menus' are lists of options, usually grouped according to general function. For example, a program's 'file' menu will let you choose from a variety of actions to do with files. Usually you move a highlight bar over the option you want – in the example above, 'Close file'.

Any program will usually have several menus, each one a list of options like this.

• **The Series 3's menus can be called up at any time simply by pressing the Menu key (bottom left of the keyboard).**

Cursor keys

Apart from giving you a list of the commands available, menus also let you select these commands very simply and quickly. Instead of typing them in wholesale, all you have to do is 'highlight' them with a special bar or cursor.

Depending on the machine, these highlighting bars are moved around either with keys or with a 'mouse'. On the Series 3, you use the cluster of arrow keys to the bottom left of the keyboard. Once highlighted, menu items are 'activated' by pressing the Enter key (to the right of the keyboard).

The Series 3 has a set of four 'cursor' keys to the bottom right of the keyboard for moving the highlighting bar around the menus (just one of their functions).

Dialogs

Menu systems are a very simple and effective way of inputting commands, but most programs are a bit too complex to have all their functions taken care of by a few short lists of commands.

The way round this is to incorporate 'dialogs'. Some menu options on the Psion are followed by a row of dots. This means that when you select them you call up a box containing another set of options.

Here, though, you may be asked to type in numbers, names or yes/no answers (hence the term 'dialog'). Dialogs are otherwise very much like menus – you use the arrow keys to select the option you want. And dialogs, like menus, tend to consist of sets of related functions. For example, the Alter

Paragraph dialog in the Word program on the Psion consists of margin settings, insets, font and typestyle settings for a given paragraph.

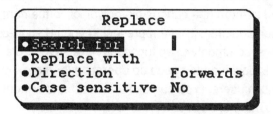

'Dialogs' often follow on from menu items (look for menu items followed by a row of dots). They let you type in the information the software needs to carry out the job. The example above is called up by the Replace option on the Scan menu in the Series 3's Word program.

In extreme cases, one option in a dialog may give rise to yet another dialog! When you're using a menu/dialog system, you do have to try to keep track of 'where you are'. Dialogs and menus are often 'nested'. Imagine main menus as forming the branches of a tree, while sub-menus and dialogs are the smaller branches, often leading to smaller branches still! (We'll resist the urge to call them twigs…)

Changing your mind

While you're finding your way around the menus on the Series 3 you may get lost! You may find yourself in the middle of a dialog you didn't want, having changed something you didn't want to change. Don't panic! The Esc key (top left-hand corner of the keyboard) is there to get you out of such sticky spots. Pressing Esc takes you out of the current menu or dialog and back to what you were doing before. That may be back to that nasty letter you were writing to the bank manager or the previous menu/dialog.

Keyboard short-cuts

Many of the options on the Psion's menus have curious 'codes' attributed to them (the curious hieroglyphics to the right of many of the menu opions). These represent keyboard short-cuts – all of the most commonly-used functions have keyboard short-cuts, and this is designed to speed up operation for more experienced users. (You can use the short-cuts without having to call up the menus at all.)

These codes consist of single letters pressed in conjunction with the special Psion key to the bottom left of the keyboard (use it like the Shift key). While the menu system is friendly, it's not particularly fast, and once you've learned the short-cuts you may abandon it altogether.

The beauty of the system is that you can learn these short-cuts at your own pace – or not at all.

Help!

Completely stuck? Well that's where this book comes in. But for those occasions when you don't have it with you, the Psion has a built-in 'Help' function. Try pressing the Help button to the bottom right of the keyboard when you get into difficulties. This presents a large dialog listing all the Help topics available. Select the one you want in the same way that you'd select a command or option – by highlighting it with the arrow keys and then pressing Enter.

Computers really *are* getting friendlier!

THE SYSTEM

The System screen is the 'nerve centre' of your Series 3. You call it up with a button, just like the built-in Word, Data, Agenda etc software, but it's more like your Series 3's worktop than a program in itself.

What the System screen gives you is a display of all the built-in programs plus all the files created with those programs. These are listed vertically below the program icons.

You also get a full set of menus allowing you to carry out a variety of general housekeeping jobs as well as more specific functions.

You can, via the System screen, do all the following:

- Rapidly select and open different files from different applications
- Create, delete, copy and rename files
- 'Customise' the machine to your own needs and preferences
- Check memory usage and battery condition
- Handle the Psion's optional plug-in 'disks'
- Create and manage 'directories' for organising large numbers of files
- Instal new applications and remove existing application icons from the display
- Define keyboard short-cuts for opening up applications

Swapping between files
One of the things you'll find yourself most often using the System screen for is selecting other files.

You can do this, of course, without using the System screen at all. If, for example, you want to move from the Agenda, where you're currently entering your day's appointments, to a Word file, you'd press the Word button. This would bring up the Word

Data

Word

Agenda

Time

World

Calc

Program

System

Data

Word

Agenda

Time

World

Calc

Program

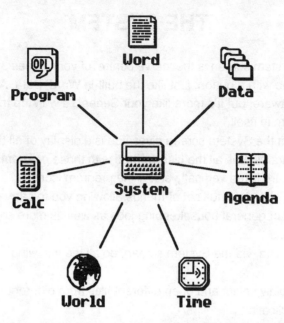

The System Screen is the nerve centre of your Series 3.
You can use it a a jumping-off point for all the built-in
applications.

file you were last working on. If this isn't the file you want, you
then have to call up the File menu, select Open File and then
choose the one you want from the list.

It's certainly easy enough, but compared to the ease with
which you can do the same thing from the System screen, it's
definitely a bit of a palaver.

Selecting applications
When you call up the System screen you'll notice that each of
the program buttons below the display is duplicated on-screen.
To select one of these programs, use the Left/Right arrow keys,
then press Enter. This opens up the file in that application you
were last working on. In this respect, the System screen works

just the same as the program buttons.

Later on, though, if you add more programs to your Series 3 (various additional programs are planned – call Psion for the latest details), this changes. Each new program will have its own icon on the System screen, whereas you obviously can't add program buttons! The System screen will be the only way of getting at any additional programs you add to the machine – unless you reconfigure the buttons (see later this chapter).

Selecting files

As well as displaying icons for all the built-in programs, the System screen lists all the files created with these programs below their respective icons. If there are too many files to display in the space, you'll have to use the Up/Down arrow keys to scroll through them all.

The file at the top of the list is the last one you were working on. This will usually be in bold, to indicate it is still 'open'. The main practical effect of this is that whenever you press the relevant program button, that's the file which will be called up.

• **You 'close' files by using the Exit command on the Special menu.**

If there is no file open for a particular program, pressing that program's button doesn't call up the program but returns you instead to the System screen, where the program icon has a list of available files below it.

To select a file from the System screen, first use the Left/Right arrows to select the right program, then use the Up/Down arrows to highlight the file you want. Now just press Enter. The file is loaded. From now on, until you use the Exit command from within that file, that's the currently 'open' file for that program.

The System screen lets you bypass these 'open' files. They are always shown in bold at the top of the list, but all you have to do is highlight another file from the list and press Enter. That

System

Data

Word

Agenda

Time

World

Calc

Program

file is then opened up, and becomes the 'open' one.

Using the System screen is a much quicker method than fiddling around with files from within a program itself, plus you get to see all the files available.

 The left/right arrow keys move you between programs

 The up/down arrow keys move you between files

You can select files direct from the System screen, rather than have to load the program they were created with and then open them from there.

Handling files

You can do much more than just view and open files from the System screen, though. Once you've highlighted the program you want, you can create, copy, delete and rename files just as easily as if you were using the program itself.

You do all this via the File menu. To try it out, first of all highlight the Agenda program. Then call up the File menu and select New File. Call the new file 'Work' and then press Enter. You'll now find a brand new Agenda file called Work has loaded, to which you can start adding all your business engagements.

You can also copy files via the System screen – useful if you want to make a 'back-up' in case you do something stupid with a very important file (like inadvertently deleting all the information, for example!).

The System screen's Copy command works in much the same way as the Save As option provided within the programs

– but it's much simpler to use. Simply highlight the relevant program for the file you want to copy and select Copy File from the File menu.

You will now be asked to choose which file you want to copy out of those created with that program (From File), and what name you want to give the copy – the machine won't let you have two files with the same name (To File).

Don't worry about the other questions in the dialog about disks, Subcirectories and Modifications – we'll come to those later. Leave these at their default settings.

To delete a file, first highlight it with the arrow keys and then select Delete from the File menu. You are asked if you're sure you want to delete the file. Are you? It's your last chance to change your mind! When you confirm the operation, the file disappears from the screen – and there's no way of getting it back.

If you want to change the name of one of your files, one way is to open in up and then Save As another filename. However, this leaves you with two copies of the file – one with the original name, one with the new one.

A quicker and neater way is to highlight the file you want on the System screen and then select the Rename File option on the File menu.

File 'attributes'

Files can have certain specific 'Attributes' which can be set by the final option on the File menu:

Read only can be used for important files that you don't want to accidentally modify or delete. In this state, a file is protected against anything except a hard reset (see the troubleshooting chapter for more information on Hard/Soft Resets).

System

Data

Word

Agenda

Time

World

Calc

Program

System

Data

Word

Agenda

Time

World

Calc

Program

Modified files are ones which have been changed since they were last 'backed up' on to a solid state disk plugged into your machine. Back-ups are a good idea because although the Psion is reliable at retaining information, accidents can happen and it's always wise to keep copies of important files somewhere else. You can back-up your files at any time – this option decides whether the Psions backs up all files, or only those that have been modified since the last time you carried out a back-up.

Hidden and **System** files are file types designated by the Psion itself. Leave these well alone unless you know exactly what you are doing (i.e. unless you are an advanced user who's progressed far beyond the standard uses for the machine).

Setting user preferences

The Series 3 can be personalised according to your own preferences and needs. Indeed, one of the first things you're advised to do when you get your machine is to key in your 'owner information'. This is the equivalent of writing your name and address in the front of a personal organiser in case you lose it. (You'll find the Set Owner option on the Info menu.) There are various other ways of setting the machine up specifically for your needs too.

```
  Set owner information
•    Owner:
•    Phone:
•    Address:
•    Address:
```

Your Series 3 can be 'personalised' in a number of ways.

34

One of the most obvious is to type in your name and address via the Set Owner option on the Info menu.

Sound

The Series 3 offers a number of different options under the general heading 'sound'. If you like, you can set up the Psion not to make a peep even when an alarm goes off (especially useful if you're attending a meeting!) – the alarm signal will still be displayed on-screen.

You can also switch off the sound completely using the Sound option on the Special menu.

'Evaluate' format

The Word, Agenda and Data programs all offer the Evaluate option, whereby you can perform calculations on-screen in the middle of working on a document or file. The results of the calculations are normally displayed to two decimal places, but you can alter this using the Evaluate Format option on the Special menu.

Printer setup

The Special menu also offers the Printer Setup option. If you use your Series 3 purely as a personal organiser, you're unlikely to want to set it up to print files, but if you do, you'll need to check the printer settings. For more information on this, see the chapter devoted to Printing.

Auto switch-off time

The Series 3 is designed to save power by switching off while you're not using it. Obviously, it would be extremely irritating if it did this after a few seconds! – the standard delay before it switches itself off is 5 minutes, but you can modify this, even switching the feature off altogether.

Call up the Special menu and select the Auto Switch Off

System

Data

Word

Agenda

Time

World

Calc

Program

option. You'll see that if you choose Yes for Auto Switch Off, you'll be able to set the delay to whatever you like in both minutes and seconds.

Password setting

If you're worried that other people might try to look at information on your Series 3, you can protect it with a password. A System password is a pretty powerful beast, though, so don't use it lightly. And don't, whatever you do, forget it.

Whenever you switch the machine on, you will be asked for your System password (only if you've set one up, of course). If you've forgotten it, you won't be able to do anything else with the machine. The only solution is a Hard Reset, and that means losing all the information stored in the machine. Eek!

If you still want to set a System password, call up the Special menu and select the Password option. You are asked to Enter a password and then Confirm it. Even when you've chosen a password, you can still elect to have the feature turned on or off (the third line in the dialog). You can change an existing password by calling up this dialog.

System passwords are displayed in an encrypted form. In fact, each character is displayed as a padlock. You can't get much more encrypted than that.

It makes it impossible to tell if you've made a typing mistake, but it also makes it impossible for anyone looking over your shoulder to see what the password is. Unless they watch your fingers on the keys, of course...

```
Enter Password:🔒🔒🔒🔒🔒🔒
```

Use passwords with care! Even when you set them up, the characters are represented by padlock symbols.
You'll need to remember the password every time you

switch on, too...

Remote link setup

This option (also on the Scan menu) switches the serial link On or Off. This is the link you use when communicating with another computer or a serial printer. The other setting – Baud Rate – is the communications *speed*. Check the documentation of the other machine to arrive at the right communications speed.

Getting 'info'

Apart from letting you alter many of the machine's defaults and set-ups, the System screen also lets you check the Psion's operating status.

For example, how old is your machine? Which version of the Series 3 operating system does it use? Most of the time this information will be irrelevant, but if it becomes apparent there's a problem with specific machines, you'll need to be able to check whether yours is one of them. And if in the future you decide to buy a plug-in program module from Psion or another supplier, you may need to check that it's compatible with your particular machine.

To check the Version, call up the Info menu and select the Version option. The Version number is then briefly displayed in the bottom right hand corner of the screen.

Memory/disk usage

Have you had a low memory message popping up on screen recently? If so, you need to do something about it. Either you must compress some of your Data and/or Agenda files, or you must throw out some older, no longer used files altogether.

But first you need to know how much space is being used by which files, don't you?

From the Info menu, select the Memory Info option. This will tell you the total quantity of memory used and how much is left

System

Data

Word

Agenda

Time

World

Calc

Program

System

Data

Word

Agenda

Time

World

Calc

Program

to spare. To find out how much each application is using, press the Left/Right arrow keys. You may be surprised! This should give you a better idea of what you can throw away.

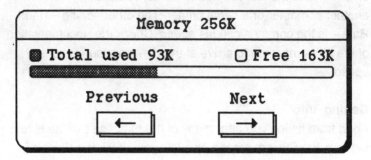

To find out how much of your Series 3's memory you've used on what, call up the Info menu and select Memory Info. The Left/Right arrow keys show you the Previous/Next info screens, which break down the memory usage according to specific programs.

Battery condition

Because of the back-up battery installed in your machine, it's very difficult to lose any information even if the main batteries fail. But if you're just about to leave on a long trip, you may want to change the batteries as a precautionary measure. To check their state of health, select the Batteries option on the Info menu.

'Solid State Disks'

Most people will be content with using just the 'Internal Disk' in the Psion. This is the machine's internal memory, enough of which is left over from its day-to-day workings for the storage of a reasonably large quantity of information.

But it may not be enough. In which case you will need to use the 'solid state' disks designed to fit into the slots on either side of the machine.

These solid state disks come in two forms: Flash SSD (Solid State Disk) or RAM SSD.

Flash SSDs work in the same way as EPROMs (Eraseable Programmable Read Only Memory). You can store files on this medium as long as you like and with total security.

You can unplug a Flash SSD and stick it in a cupboard for years, if you like, and the data will be secure. HOWEVER, it doesn't work like ordinary memory. You can't delete the information you've saved and use the space to store something else.

You can only erase the whole thing at once, and then only by a special process. Normal EPROMs have to be exposed to ultra-violet light for a certain period of time. Psion Flash SSDs, however, can be reformatted on your machine.

RAM SSDs work just like the memory inside the machine. You can continually re-use the memory by erasing old information...

BUT, like the internal memory, they need a constant supply of power to retain the data. When they're plugged into the Series 3, RAM SSDs take their power from the machine's batteries. When they're removed, they get their power from their own built-in batteries. These batteries have enough power to keep your data safe for up to a year.

Both types of SSD can be protected using their 'write protect' switches. With these switched On, files on the disks can be examined, but they can't be amended or deleted.

Directories

If you don't have any SSDs plugged into your machine, life is pretty simple. If you do, it's slightly more complicated. You are now using additional 'devices' or 'drives'. By default, the Psion's built-in memory is the 'Internal drive'. One SSD will correspond

System

Data

Word

Agenda

Time

World

Calc

Program

to 'Drive A' and a second will correspond to 'Drive B'.

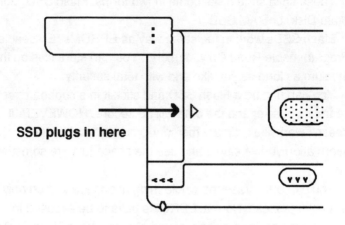

SSD plugs in here

If you turn your Series 3 over you'll find two doors on the underside which swing outwards. SSDs are plugged into the slots exposed and then the doors closed again.

For most purposes, this simple level of organisation will be all you need to get used to. However, more advanced users may want to use the Psion's directory structures. These work in the same way as those on a PC. At the simplest level, all you have to remember is the drive you've stored your file on, but if you want your storage system to be more structured, here's how it works:

Each drive, or device, has a root directory. Within this directory are various subdirectories. The Psion creates these automatically to store the different file types produced by the different programs. You can also produce your own subdirectories.

Directories and subdirectories are prefaced by a backslash (\) character. The full directory name of a file would be in the form \DAT\WORK\REPORT, for example.

40

Another feature of PCs also used by the Series 3 is 'file extensions'. These are three-letter codes separated from the filename by a dot, and which describe the file type. So an Agenda file, for example, might be ROD.AGN, even though you only need to know the filename is ROD.

Most users will never have anything to do with the Series 3's DOS-style directory and file-naming system – it's designed to be invisible in use. Simply remember that if you have one or more SSDs installed in your machine, you will need to specify which drive a file is on when you open it using a program's Open File dialog.

'Default disk'

The Series 3 automatically tries to load from and save to its internal memory – it's 'internal drive'. If you have an SSD fitted you may want to make this the default drive instead. You do this from the System screen, via the Default Disk option on the Disk menu.

Formatting disks

The only way to reclaim space on a Flash SSD is to reformat it completely. Call up the Disk menu and select the Format disk option. You can now specify the disk you want to format.

Both RAM SSDs and the machine's internal drive can also be reformatted in this way, although with these it's possible to delete files individually too (which is what you're more likely to do unless you're having a wholesale clear-out).

• **If you do have to reformat a disk, make VERY sure you're formatting the right one. Data can't be recovered if you make a mistake!**

Applications

The Series 3's internal applications (programs) each have their

System

Data

Word

Agenda

Time

World

Calc

Program

41

System

Data

Word

Agenda

Time

World

Calc

Program

own icon (symbol) on the System screen, which is identical to the one on the buttons directly below the display. Now while you obviously can't change the order of these buttons, you can change the order of the displayed icons (you're bound to use some applications more than others, and they can't all be displayed simultaneously – the screen isn't wide enough).

To change the order, call up the Apps menu and select the Install Standard option. First select the application you want to reposition, then press the Down arrow to move to the line below to adjust the position. This can either be Current (where it is at the moment), First on the list or Last.

You can do more than just change the order, though. You can also Remove applications (also on the Apps menu). This does NOT delete them from the machine's memory. Instead, it just removes their icon from the System screen. Using the Install Standard option, you can re-insert their icons at will.

If you remove an icon when one of that application's files has note been closed, the application icon will still disappear but you will get a RunIMG icon instead (a RunOPL icon if you deleted the OPL icon). This too can be deleted or repositioned. Or you can prevent it happening in the first place by making sure that you have Quit the application (also on the Apps menu).

The built-in programs are not necessarily the only ones you will ever use, though. As other programs become available, these can be added later via the Install application option on the Apps menu. Here you specify a disk and a program name.

Finally, so that you don't have to return to the System screen to open up a different application, you can assign keyboard short-cuts to your applications. This won't be necessary if you use only the internal applications supplied, since these have their own buttons. But it can be very useful for new programs.

Say, for example, you have bought a spreadsheet program for your Series 3. First of all, open the application you want to assign a button to. Now, from the System screen call up the

Apps menu and select Assign Button. You will see that all the

Word Data Agenda Time World Calc

The program buttons below the display need not necessarily call up the programs they describe. These buttons can be 'reassigned'.

labelled buttons below the display can be reassigned to this application. If you still want each button to call up its labelled application when pressed, make sure that you have used the Control modifier (second line of the dialog). This means your new key command will involve holding down the Control key and then pressing the chosen button. In this way, for example, the Agenda button on its own can still call up the Agenda program, but Control + Agenda can call up your spreadsheet program.

System

Data

Word

Agenda

Time

World

Calc

Program

43

THE DATABASE

Can you remember all your friends' telephone numbers? You can? Well, that's not bad. OK then, how about your bank's? Your insurance company's? How about those of your work colleagues, business contacts and all your clients? Quite. Sooner or later we all have to start keeping a 'phone book...

But 'phone books get filled up. Pages fall out, entries become illegible, you forget whether you stored a number according to its owner's company name, last name or first name, and so on.

The Series 3's Data software makes storing all these personal details easy. But it is also capable of storing more varied information – as much as any computerised 'database'.

A database is a piece of software that lets you save information about anything you like – people's 'phone numbers, addresses of clients, latin names of houseplants – anything. You can then recall information at will.

Usually, the information will be stored in a specific form. For example, the name of a plant, its lifespan, whether it flowers, the temperatures it will grow in.

You then find the information or the entry you want by searching for a particular keyword. For example, if you want to find out which plants will flower in the summer, you might search for the phrase 'summer flowering'. The program will then find every record which includes the phrase 'summer flowering'. Some database programs will let you search for more than one keyword at once. For example, you might want to look up all 'summer-flowering' plants that are also 'perennial'. This is getting a bit more complicated.

The Data software
There are various types of database, exhibiting different degrees of sophistication. The most powerful are expensive and

System

Data

Word

Agenda

Time

World

Calc

Program

will run only on the most hi-tech hardware.

.At the other end of the scale are simpler, 'card-index' style databases that work just like an office filing system. This is the type the Psion offers.

The analogy with an office filing system is a good one, because the Psion's database screen looks just like a small filing card. It stores half a dozen different items of information (or 'fields', to use the technical term) on each card (or 'record').

Every time you want to add a record to your filing system you create a new card and fill it in. Every time you want to find a record (you could specify a person's first name, last name, address etc) the software will flick through the cards, finding every one with the specified word (or words) on it.

• **The Series 3's Data program stores information as records in the computerised equivalent of a card index file. Each card contains the same type of information – the supplied file lets you store an individual's name, home and work telephone numbers, address and notes in specific 'fields'. You can design your own 'cards', though.**

'Save' mode

The Data software on the Series 3 works in two distinct 'modes' – the 'Save' mode and the 'Find' mode. The first is used for adding new records or updating existing information. The second is used for recalling information.

When you first press the Data button to enter the database program, you automatically enter the Save mode. The screen shows you an empty record card with 'Name', 'Home telephone'. 'Work telephone', 'Address' and 'Notes' arranged down the left hand side of the screen.

Inserting information

When this screen first comes up, you will see a cursor flashing at the start of the first line. When you start typing, text will

46

appear at this point. The cursor moves along, staying to the right of your text.

Try typing someone's name. When you've finished, press Enter (or Down arrow) and you're then on the next line – Home telephone number. Type that in and press Enter to move on to the next line.

Ah, but what if you don't have a Work telephone number? No problem – just press Enter straight away. You move on to the Address line, leaving the previous one blank.

When you type in the address, you'll note that (a) it's given two lines on the screen and (b) if you keep typing the line just scrolls along as you meet the edge of the screen! That second Address line can only be reached by pressing Enter again, otherwise the address goes all on one line and you have to use the arrow keys to read it all. If you press Enter as you near the edge of the screen, though, while typing in the address, you start the second line – you may be able to get the whole of the address on-screen at once this way.

'Notes' only gets one line, but you can carry on pressing Enter to get extra lines at will.

Maximum entry size
However, you can't go on typing indefinitely. Although you can make each line as long as you like, it has to be within a maximum limit of 4096 characters for the whole record. One letter is a single character, so that equates to roughly 800-900 words. That should be enough for most purposes!

When you've finished typing in your record, press the Tab key to save it (a big message is continuously displayed at the bottom of the screen – "Press Tab to save entry").

Editing information
So far so good. But what if you realise you've made a mistake typing in your record? No problem, because as long as you

haven't saved it you can go back and fix it. You move the cursor keys about using the arrow keys, and press Delete to take out the offending text. Then you can simply type in what you meant to write.

The editing functions are a bit more sophisticated than that, though. In fact, you have the same set of controls as the Word program offers.

For a start, if using the arrow keys is too slow for you, try holding down the Control key at the same time:

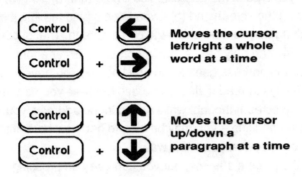

For moving around even faster, use the Psion key:

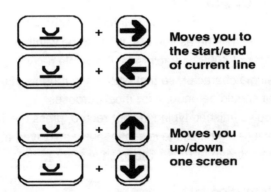

You can also move straight to the start or end of the record with:

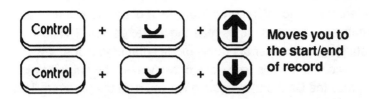

Moves you to the start/end of record

It is also possible to select whole areas of text to delete at once, rather than having to use the Delete key repeatedly. Just place the cursor where you want the highlighting to start, then keep the Shift key pressed as you move to where you want it to end. Press Delete when you've highlighted all the text you want to discard and it's gone!

You use the same method to highlight text you want to copy to another place in that record or even another record entirely. You delete it as before, but then place the cursor where you want to move it to and select the Insert Text option on the Edit menu.

• **When you Delete highlighted text, the Series 3 wipes it from the screen but 'remembers' it. When you select Insert Text, the 'remembered' text is pasted in.**

You might not want to move a section of text but instead make a copy of it to place somewhere else. For this, highlight the text and then select the Copy option on the Edit menu – don't press Delete. Now move the cursor to the point where you want the copied text to be inserted and select Insert Text, as before.

There is another option on the Edit menu – Bring Text. This works much like the Insert Text option, except that with this you can copy in text from another one of the Series 3's built-in programs. For example, you could select some text in the Word program, press the Data button to enter the database, move the cursor to the appropriate point and select Bring Text to import that text into one of your database records.

System

Data

Word

Agenda

Time

World

Calc

Program

System Data Word Agenda Time World Calc Program

'Find' mode

Entering and storing records is only part of the work of a database. The main part is recalling these records. This is the Data program's other operating mode – the Find mode.

You can enter this mode one of two ways. The quick way is to press the Data button again once you're in the program. This acts as a toggle between the Save and Find modes. Press it again to get back to Save mode.

The other way is via the menus. Call up the Search Menu and select Find to enter Find mode.

When you're in the Find mode there's a window at the bottom of the screen where you can type in text – the Data program finds the records you want by first asking you for a phrase to find. This can be a word, a series of words or a part of a word.

• **The Word software asks you to specify whether you want the search to be 'case-sensitive'. In other words, whether you want it to take account of capital letters or not. You don't get this option with the Data software (nor do you need it really) so it makes no difference whether you search for 'Griselda', 'griselda' or 'GRISELDA', you will still find every record containing the unfortunate girl's name.**

The program will now find the first record containing your specified text.

To see if there is more than one, press Enter again and the program will search for the next record containing that text... and so on until there are no more records to search.

It may be, however, that you don't want to search out specific records, merely browse through all the records in sequence. This is easy. Just delete any text in the Find window, leaving it empty, then press Enter. You've specified nothing, so the program calls up every record in turn, allowing you to examine each one.

You aren't limited to going forwards through your recordseither. Press Shift+Return to go backwards.

System

Data

Word

Agenda

Time

World

Calc

Program

```
   Name: Barney Bear
   Home: 010 463 777 29106
   Work: 010 463 777 29107
1  Address: Bear House, Bear
            Avenue, Bearsville
   Notes: A bit hairy

   Find:
```

```
   Name: Donald Duck
   Home: 010 463 777 29103
   Work: 010 463 777 29104
2  Address: Duck House, Duck
            Road, Ducksville
   Notes: Likes water

   Find: duck
```

When you're in the Data program's Find mode, you type in the text you want to search for at the cursor in the small window at the bottom of the display (1). When a match has been found, the appropriate record is displayed (2).

• **The Find, Find Again and Find Previous options can all be found on the Search menu, but there seems little point calling this up when it's so easy to search through using the Enter and Shift+Enter commands.**

When you find the record you're searching for it may look slightly different to when you typed it in. This is because of the limited size of the display – the program makes the most of it by

51

cutting out all blank lines. If you left out a work phone number, for example, there will not be a work phone number line at all when you recall the record.

Sometimes a record will be too long or too wide to fit on the screen. When you find a record like this, use the arrow keys to scroll the screen to see the hidden text.

Editing existing records

Earlier on we looked at how to edit records before you saved them. What if you want to alter a record that's already *been* saved? You can do this by first finding the record you want to change and then calling up the Change menu and selecting the Update option. This puts you back into the Save mode, but instead of giving you a blank screen for a new record, you get to edit the current record, just as if you'd typed it in but hadn't pressed Tab to save it yet.

The Change menu also has the following options: Enter Data (the same as just switching back to Save mode with the Data button) and Delete (you can also Delete simply by pressing the Delete key having found a record). Delete, in the Find mode, means to delete an entire record.

Labels

The Series 3's built-in data file is a simple address book. And each line (or set of lines) has a label. But you can do more with the Data program than just store names and addresses! These labels can be changed to whatever you like.

In normal use you don't alter the labels, only the text that follows them. However, you can edit the existing labels or create new labels.

First of all, create a new file by calling up the File menu and selecting New File. This will give you a blank file. It is still set up to store names and addresses, but we can change all that...

• **Take care when you're editing the labels in a database**

System

Data

Word

Agenda

Time

World

Calc

Program

file already containing records. You can move the labels about, or change the number of lines they take up, but the information you've stored won't move with them! If you're not careful, your labels end up out of step with the information they're supposed to relate to.

Call up the Special menu and select Edit Labels. You can now edit all the labels, pressing Enter to add blank lines if you think the information may take up quite a lot of space.

Labels —

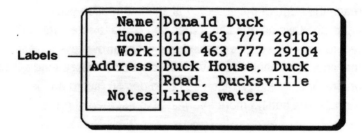

```
    Name:Donald Duck
    Home:010 463 777 29103
    Work:010 463 777 29104
 Address:Duck House, Duck
        Road, Ducksville
   Notes:Likes water
```

You're not stuck with the Psion's standard 'phone book style database. By choosing your own labels, you can create files to store any information you like.

You can duplicate the phone symbol used by the built-in database by pressing Shift+Psion+Help. This is more than purely cosmetic, since it tells the machine that the following number can be dialled – very useful when you want to auto-dial telephone numbers (see later).
• Although the data you enter subsequently can be pretty well any length, the labels themselves can't. About half a screen width is all you're allowed.

Hiding/showing labels
You may decide, once you've typed in all your records, that the labels just get in the way and you don't want to see them any more. To hide them, call up the Special menu and select Hide

Labels. To bring them back, call up the Special menu again. This time the option will have changed to Show Labels.

Word-wrap

The Word software automatically starts you on a new line whenever you reach the edge of the display as you type. The Data software doesn't. At least, it doesn't unless you want it to.

There are advantages to having word-wrap switched off. You keep on typing and the text starts scrolling to the left once you reach the edge of the screen – all the information you're inputting stays on one line. When you come to re-examine the record you have to use the Left and Right arrow keys to read that line. This means that even the longest addresses etc still fit on one line, making it much easier to design record and label formats and getting more information on-screen at once.

```
          Name: Donald Duck
          Home: 010 463 777 29103
          Work: 010 463 777 29104
    1  Address: Duck House, Duck
                Road, Ducksville
         Notes: Likes water
```

```
          Name: Donald Duck
          Home: 010 463 777 29103
          Work: 010 463 777 29104
    2  Address: Duck House, Duck Rc

         Notes: Likes water
```

If you have Word Wrap switched On (1), longer entries like addresses will automatically 'wrap' on to the next line.

54

System

Data

Switch Word Wrap Off, though, (2) and the text disappears out of the side of the window. However, this does mean you can get each field on a single line.

You can make up your own mind about word wrapping by calling up the Special menu and selecting the Wrap On/Off function. Try them both and see which you prefer.

Notes

A database record doesn't have to consist of a rigidly-designed set of facts. The standard data file that comes with the machine has a space for notes at the bottom of the record, and you can use this for any information that doesn't really fit into any of the other categories.

But you can take this one stage further by setting up a database which consists of nothing *but* notes. You can then use the Find mode to look for specific keywords. For example, you might want to store personal summaries of your clients or employees. The information doesn't have to be properly structured in a database-style format.

Handling Data files

You can create any number of files with the Data program. Each Data 'file' is a collection of records you can add to at will. Each file can have its own record layout and labels. You edit or search or add to a Data file by first 'opening' it.

There are two ways of doing this:

1) Press the System button to return to the System screen. Then use the arrow keys to highlight the required file from the list under the Data symbol. Press Enter and the currently active Data file we be closed and the one you selected opened.

2) Call up the File menu and select the Open File option. Use the Left and Right arrow keys to choose the file you want, then

Word

Agenda

Time

World

Calc

Program

press Enter to close the current file and open the selected one.

You can create an entirely new Data file by again calling up the File menu but this time selecting the New File option. This will give you a replica of the standard name-and-address file which you can then modify at will.

If you don't want to use this standard Data file format as a starting point, there is another way – load up another Data file and call up the File menu. Select the Save As option and save the file under the new name. You now have two copies of that file – the original, which is now closed, and a copy. You can then use this copy as the basis for your new file.

This Save As dialog has a couple of other bits and pieces in it, though. We'll ignore the Disk type, since we're assuming you're working with the standard internal memory. But what's this Data or Text option below?

Well, the standard format for your information is Data. Data files are the ones that you load up with Open File. However, you can also save your information as plain text, for loading into the Word program, for example. If you do this, you need a thing called a Delimiter Code.

A Delimiter Code is what marks the end of the fields in each record. You have two choices, really. You can have each field starting on a new line, or you can have them one after the other on the same line, so that each record takes up just a single line when 'imported' into your Word document. It really depends on what you want to do with the data. If all you want to do is print it out, then the Newline option is probably the best.

If, however, you want to transfer your Data file to another computer, for use in another database, you will need this Delimiter Code to 'tell' that computer's software where one field ends and another begins. Different programs use different Delimiter Codes, so you'll have to check the other software's instructions. Whatever it is, it will either be offered as one of the alternative options to 'Newline' or you can select Other and then define it yourself on the line below.

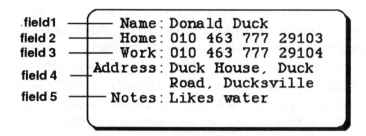

.field1 —— Name: Donald Duck
field 2 —— Home: 010 463 777 29103
field 3 —— Work: 010 463 777 29104
field 4 —— Address: Duck House, Duck
                     Road, Ducksville
field 5 —— Notes: Likes water

You can transfer Data files from the Series 3 to a desktop computer. But make sure you know how the other machine's software tells one field (name, telephone number, address etc) from another. Some programs expect each field to be on a new line, others expect commas between fields and so on.

If you're Saving As using the standard Data format, the last option in the dialog will let you choose between using the new file you've just created or sticking with the old one. Make sure you always know which file you're editing!

'Merging' files

You can 'add' Data files together by using the Merge In option on the File menu. When you 'Merge In', the Data file you merge is added to the end of the one currently open. This feature is useful if you've built up several Data files on clients and business contacts, for example, and you want to combine them into one big database.

Be warned, though – the separate Data files must always have the same format and labels. It's the file you're *merging into* that decides the format, and if the files you're *merging in* aren't laid out the same way, you're going to get some pretty weird results. In other words, unless you've made sure all the Data

System

Data

Word

Agenda

Time

World

Calc

Program

files are identical in layout/labelling, don't try it.

The Merge In dialog is pretty much identical to the Save As dialog. Instead of typing in your own filename, however, you're given a list of those available for Merging In. Apart from that, though, you can again choose to work with Data or Text files. There's little point in merging in another Data file as text, though, especially if you don't use the Newline delimiter code. In this case, the software will try to load the new records into a single line, for which they will almost certainly be too long.

Copying text

You can copy and move text from either another part of the current record or another record quite easily using the Copy/Insert Text option on the Edit menu.

First find the record you want to copy/move from. Then call up the Change menu and select the Update option.

• **Remember, the Update option always enables you to edit existing records. You'll soon remember its keyboard shortcut for extra sped too.**

Now use the Shift+arrow keys to highlight the text you want to Move or Copy.

If you want to move it, press Delete. The text disappears, but it has been saved temporarily in the machine's memory. To re-insert the text in another part of that record, move the cursor to the appropriate position, call up the Edit menu and select the Insert Text option.

To place the text in another record, you will first have to leave the current one by pressing Tab to save the changes. Once you've done that, you'll be back in the Find mode. It's then possible to paste the text into another record.

Find the record you want to place the text in, select Update from the Change menu and then put the cursor where you want the text to fall.

Again, use the Insert Text option on the Edit menu.

58

```
┌─────────────────────────────────────┐
│     Name: Donald Duck                │
│     Home: 010 463 777 29103          │
│     Work: 010 463 777 29104          │
│  Address: Duck House   Duck          │
│           Road, Ducksville           │
│    Notes: Likes water                │
└─────────────────────────────────────┘
```

You can copy text from one part of a record to another, or from one record to another and even from one Data file to another. You can even copy chunks of text from one Series 3 program to another. All you have to do is highlight the text with the Shift + Arrow keys.

You're not limited to moving text around within single Data files, either. Once you've Copied or Deleted your highlighted text, you can return to the System screen and select another Data file entirely. Open this file, select the record you want to add the text to, as before, and Bob's your uncle!

Pasting in text from another program entirely is only marginally more difficult. For this you need to first select the file you want to transfer text *from* – for example, a Word file. Highlight the text you want to transfer, using the Shift+arrow keys as usual, then return to your Data file. Choose the spot where you want to insert the text, call up the Edit menu and this time select the Bring Text option.

You can copy a Data file by selecting Save As from the File menu. Give it a different name and choose whether you want to continue working on either the new file or the old one.

Deleting records
To delete a record in a Data file, call up the Change menu and

System

Data

Word

Agenda

Time

World

Calc

Program

select Delete.

To delete an entire Data file, you'll need to first press the System button. Call up the File menu and select the Delete option. You will now get a list of all the Data files you have (if you get Word files or Agenda files instead you've got the wrong program highlighted on the System screen – press Esc and make sure you move the cursor to the right one this time!). Choose the file you want to delete using the Left/Right arrows, then press Enter.

The machine now asks you if you're sure. Well, are you...?

Compacting your database

As your database grows and develops you'll find yourself not only adding records but deleting records too. When you delete a record, though, the machine can't immediately reclaim that memory space. Instead, deleting a record just leaves a 'hole'. A similar thing happens when you *edit* an existing entry. Space is still taken up by the 'old' version, once you've saved the new one.

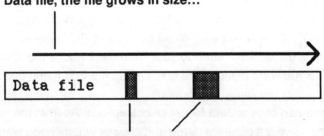

As you add information to your Data file, the file grows in size...

`Data file`

...but deleting information doesn't reduce the file size again. Instead, it just leaves 'gaps'

If your Series 3 ever runs out of available memory, the first thing you should do to free some memory up is compress any Data files you've got stored.

Now and again it's good practice to clear up these 'holes' by using the Compress option on the File menu.

Printing
To find out how to set up a printer with the Series 3, check the relevant chapter in this book. But to find out how to print out Data files with this printer, read on...

The first thing to do is to make sure you're in the Find mode, otherwise you won't be able to print. The next job (you should only have to do this once) is to select the Print Setup dialog from the Special menu, just to make sure your basic print settings are correct.

The options you're given are as follows:

Page Size – A range of preset sizes is available (scroll through the list with the Left/Right arrow keys, or you can define your own page size by moving the cursor down to the lines below and typing in your own values. The last option, Orientation, lets you decide whether the paper should be printed on 'sideways' or 'lengthways'.

Margins – These represent the clear space left around the borders of your paper. You can set these manually to whatever you like, as long as they're not so narrow the printer can't handle the paper properly or not so wide that they meet in the middle of the sheet!

Headers and Footers – These are lines of text that you can arrange to have printed at the tops/bottoms of successive pages. They can contain information like the page number, or the name of the file. See the more complete description in the

System

Data

Word

Agenda

Time

World

Calc

Program

Word section of this book.

Paging Control – This is for when you have a Header or Footer containing the page number. Do you want to the numbering to start at 1? If not, change it here. Do you want Data records to be split between pages if they fall at the end of a sheet? No? Decide here. Finally, you can choose whether the pages are numbered with the traditional Arabic numbers or lower/upper case Roman numerals.

Printer Model – The Series 3 is originally set up to work with the Canon BJ-10e bubble jet machine, but other machines are also catered for – yours may be on the list in this dialog. If not, don't worry – the Series 3 will work with just about every other printer in common use. See the section on printing for more detailed information.

Having got this out of the way, you're now ready to print. Call up the File menu and select Print. This gives you the Print To Parallel dialog, which contains the following options:

New Page For Each Entry – Unless your records are particularly large, or you're feeling particularly wasteful, set this to No.

Entries – Do you want to print all the records in the file? Do you only want to print those matching with text/numbers you've just fed into the Find option? Do you only want to print the record currently displayed? Choose here.

Pages – Do you want to print all pages or only some? (This applies if you've previously printed out the whole file and just want to update one or two pages, for example.)

Show Blank Lines – The Data software doesn't display blank lines, since that would waste space. Normally, the machine doesn't print them, either. If you want to print blank lines, though, choose Yes here.

Keep Entries Together – Normally this would be set to No.

• **Data files are usually printed with their labels. If you don't want the labels printed, make sure you have selected Hide Labels on the Special menu before you start.**
• **The special 'phone' symbol used by the Psion to indicate a telephone number won't print out. Instead, the machine converts it to another character that the printer can handle.**

Dialling

These natty little 'phone symbols that the Data software uses in its labels are more than cosmetic. They indicate to the software that what follows is a number that can be dialled.

You see the Series 3 can dial telephone numbers for you if you have a tone-dialling 'phone. All you have to do is hold the receiver by the machine's speaker grille!

System

Data

Word

Agenda

Time

World

Calc

Program

The Series 3's auto-dialling function (tone-dialling 'phones only) means you may never have to tap out a number again!

First of all, though, you've got to set the machine up correctly (although most of the standard settings won't need changing). To do this you'll have to press the World button. Now call up the Dial menu and select Defaults (well, it is the only option on the menu!).

The first thing you have to check is the Dial Out Code. If you work in an office the chances are that your calls have to be prefixed with a '9' in order to go through the switchboard. If not, you can change it here.

Have you set the right home country? If you've already set up your Home City, you won't need to change this unless you work in a different country (now that would be *real* commuting...).

The Tone Time, Delay Time and Pause Time can almost certainly be left as they are. Only if you have trouble getting your phone to work with the Psion's auto-dialling should you start messing with these. Tone Time refers to the duration of each tone, Delay Time is the delay between each tone and Pause Time is an extra delay provided by a comma. You may have to introduce an extra pause after dialling "9" for an outside call, for example.

Now you're ready to go! Have you got a Data file containing telephone numbers? Good. Open it up, Find a record and then press Psion+Help. You will now get a dialog containing every telephone number in that record. Use the Up/Down arrow keys to select the number you want to dial, then press:

Esc – if you've changed your mind and want to abandon the operation

Menu – if you want Free-form Dialling (the machine dials the numbers you type in)

Tab – to dial

Enter – to dial out via your company's switchboard (the number will be prefixed by a "9", or whatever dial-out code you specified when setting up for dialling in World.

International calls
The Psion doesn't just stop at that. It can use the information in World in conjunction with your Home City information to let you make international calls from anywhere in the World with the correct international dialling codes...

It's not just a case of typing full international codes into your Data files, you see. This will work from this country, but if you were to try dialling these numbers while abroad, things would go hopelessly wrong – what might be the correct international dialling code for, say, Denmark from the UK would probably call up Jacques' Patisserie round the corner if you tried dialling it from Paris.

Instead, you should type in international numbers *without* either the international access code or that country's own code. In other words store the number just as it would be dialled if you were already in that country.

Having done that, you need to attach the name of the country after the number. You can do this easily by first moving the cursor to the end of the number then pressing Shift+Control+Psion+Help. This gives you the Append Country dialog, and you can scroll through the list available with the Left/Right arrow keys. Found the one you want? Press Enter and the the name of the country is added in square brackets.

There's just one more thing to remember. When you go abroad, reset the Home City in World to the nearest one on the list. Do this, and you can dial anywhere in the world with your

System

Data

Word

Agenda

Time

World

Calc

Program

existing stock of numbers – the Series 3 will automatically work out the correct international code for calls from the country you're in to the country you're calling.

Evaluate

The Evaluate function is a simple mathematical tool available in the Word and Agenda software too. Basically it lets you perform simple calculations within records.

For example, if you type "21/7", then place the cursor anywhere within that calculation and select Evaluate from the Edit menu, the machine will display an 'equals' sign and the answer immediately afterwards. For this to work there must be no spaces within the calculation. If there are spaces you need to highlight the whole calculation (Shift+arrow keys) and then select Evaluate.

THE WORD PROCESSOR

What's the difference between a pen and paper and a typewriter? Exactly – a typewriter makes the scrawlings of the most untidy writer look clean and legible. The word processor does much the same with the intellectual process...

Both typewriters and word processors let you produce readable, professional-looking writing, but the advantage of the word processor is that you can view what you've written, edit, reorganise and rewrite it before you ever take that momentous step of committing it to paper.

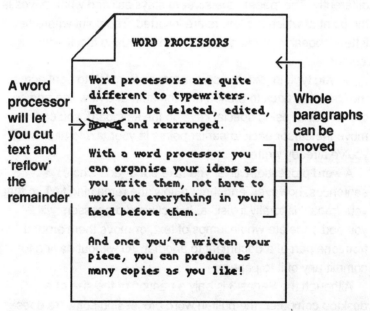

A word processor will let you cut text and 'reflow' the remainder

WORD PROCESSORS

Word processors are quite different to typewriters. Text can be deleted, edited, ~~moved~~ and rearranged.

With a word processor you can organise your ideas as you write them, not have to work out everything in your head before them.

And once you've written your piece, you can produce as many copies as you like!

Whole paragraphs can be moved

Word processors are a writer's dream. You can cut, copy, rearrange, edit, and print out your text as much as you like!

Writing made easy?
Computers make writing very much easier in a practical sense,

(Side tabs: System, Data, Word, Agenda, Time, World, Calc, Program)

67

System   Data   Word   Agenda   Time   World   Calc   Program

too. You don't have to keep winding in fresh sheets of paper, the keyboard is much quieter (and you don't get the sheer racket of strikers hitting paper) and you don't even have to bother with carriage returns at the end of each line – computer software can work out when a word is too long to fit on the end of a line and start the next line automatically. You can also adjust the layout of your document *after* you've finished writing. Finally, each word-processed document is saved as a 'file' which you can then print out as many times as you like.

With a typewriter, the letters always strike in the same place, it's just the paper that moves. Computer word processors work differently. The 'paper' (the screen) stays still and what moves is the point at which the letters are inserted. The point where new letters appear is marked usually with a flashing block – the 'cursor'.

As you type in text, the cursor moves from left to right across the line, then back to the left and the start of a new line and so on. However, using special keys on the keyboard, you can move the cursor back to earlier points in your text to alter what you've already written.

A word processor will let you take out or add whole sentences, however, and then 'reflow' the remaining text so that your 'repair' is totally invisible. In fact word processors will let you add or delete whole lumps of text, or move them around from one part of a document to another. All without having to commit any of it to paper.

Although the Series 3 is only a fraction of the size of a desktop computer, the built-in word processing software does pretty well everything you would expect from a much larger machine. Indeed, the printed output is indistinguishable from that you'd get from an office PC.

There are drawbacks, however. The small keyboard on the Psion means that touch-typing is out of the question. Two-finger typists will find it just as quick as a larger keyboard, but faster typists will find it slows them down.. Also, the smaller screen size compared to that of a desktop machine means that you can see much less of your document at any one time.

However, you can't put a desktop machine in your pocket! Neither can you use any other machine while standing up (waiting for a train, perhaps). In this respect the Series 3 is unique – a machine offering full word-processing functions that will slip into your pocket.

Starting up Word

There are two ways of opening up a word processor document onthe Psion:

(a) You can simply press the special Word button whatever you are currently doing – this opens up the last Word document you were working on. If no documents exist, you are given a blank screen to start typing on.

(b) If your machine already has one or more Word documents stored on it, and you want to open one in particular, first press the System button. This displays icons for all of the Series 3's programs – Data, Word, Agenda and so on – together with a list of any files created with them (displayed beneath each one). To select the one you want, use the arrow keys to the bottom right of the keyboard to highlight your choice. Now simply press the Enter key, and the file will be opened.

Editing text

If you haven't got a document (file) to play around with yet, just write some text for sample purposes. It doesn't matter what, but see if you can make it a few paragraphs long.

All done?

OK, now try using the arrow keys again. Notice how the cursor (the flashing block) moves up or down a line when you use the Up or Down arrows, and left or right a letter when you use the Left or Right arrows.

System

Data

Word

Agenda

Time

World

Calc

Program

System Data Word Agenda Time World Calc Program

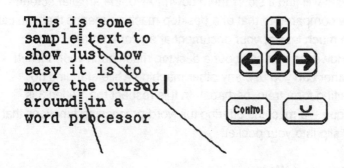

```
This is some
sample text to
show just how
easy it is to
move the cursor
around in a
word processor
```

You use the arrow keys to move the cursor to any point in your text. The Control and Psion keys let you move it in larger 'jumps'.

If you keep pressing these arrow keys you can move to any part of the document that you want. However, this could take a little while, especially with larger documents. Which is why there are various short-cuts you can use to get to where you want to go quicker.

• **The words 'document' and 'file' can be taken to mean the same thing here. 'File' is the generic term for any single item stored by a computer; 'document' usually refers simply to a text 'file'.**

Look for the Control key to the far left of the keyboard. This key works just like the Shift key – holding it down while you press another key gives you a different effect. The Shift key will give you capital letters, but the Control key does something different. Holding down Control and then pressing the Up arrow moves the cursor up to the start of the paragraph (or the *previous* paragraph if you're already at the start of one). Similarly, pressing Control+Down arrow moves the cursor to the end of the current paragraph. (Again, if it's already at the end of a paragraph, it moves to the end of the next one.) Pressing Control and the Left or Right arrows moves the cursor left and

70

right whole words, rather than whole letters, at a time.

You can move around even quicker than this, though. The Psion key, right at the bottom left of the keyboard, works like the Control and Shift keys – you hold it down while you press other keys. And you get another set of effects when you use the Psion and arrow keys together. Pressing Psion+Up arrow moves the cursor up by one screenful of text, Psion+Down arrow moves it down a screen. Pressing Psion+Left/Right arrow moves the cursor either to the start or the end of the line.

And that's not all! You can use the Control and Psion keys together – Control+Psion+Up arrow takes the cursor right back to the start of the document, while Control+Psion+Down arrow takes it to the very end.

To summarise, then, here are all the cursor control commands:

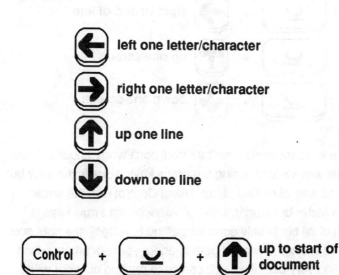

← **left one letter/character**

→ **right one letter/character**

↑ **up one line**

↓ **down one line**

Control + ⌣ + ↑ **up to start of document**

Control + ⌣ + ↓ **down to end of document**

System

Data

Word

Agenda

Time

World

Calc

Program

System Data **Word** Agenda Time World Calc Program

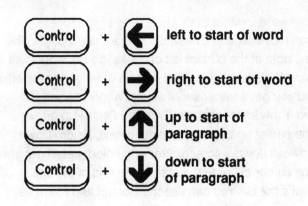

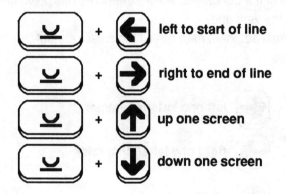

Quite a lot to memorise, isn't it? Well don't worry about it. Think of it this way instead. Using the arrow keys alone is the slow but 'detailed' way of getting about. Using Control with the arrow keys is faster but cruder. Using Psion with the arrow keys is fastest of all but is only good for getting to *roughly* the right spot.

There is another way of getting about your document which you'll find very useful when it comes to printing out your work. This is the 'Jump to Page' command.

Because the Series 3 has only a small screen, it cannot display lines of text as they would appear when printed on A4 paper. However, the machine can still calculate where pages would begin on paper, and will let you jump to these page beginnings.

First of all though, your document must obviously be long enough to take up more than one sheet of paper. That being the case, press the Menu key to bring up the Word program's menu system. Now use the Left or Right arrow keys to get to the Scan menu. Now use the Down arrow key to select the Jump to Page option. Press Enter, and the machine will briefly calculate the page positions, then produce a window displaying a page number. Use the arrow keys to change this page number to the one you want to jump to.

If the number won't change it's because your document only has one page! Similarly, you can't get the number to go below one or above the last page number of your document – the Psion already has these worked out.

Deleting text

Well we've spent long enough finding out how to move the cursor about a document – what do you do when you get it to the right spot? Let's assume that you're trying to correct a mistake. For this you need the Delete key to the top right of the keyboard. Pressing Delete rubs out the letter or character immediately to the left of the cursor. Keep pressing it and it keeps deleting characters, so don't get carried away!

If deleting *previous* characters like this is too confusing for you, try using Shift+Delete. This deletes *forward* of the cursor position – i.e. to the right of the cursor.

Using the Delete key like this is fine for minor spelling mistakes, but it's a bit slow if you want to take out larger chunks of text. For this you need to 'highlight' the offending text and then delete it.

Try this: move the cursor to the end of a word you want to delete. Now instead of pressing Delete repeatedly, hold down Shift and then press the Left arrow. Aha – something strange is

System

Data

Word

Agenda

Time

World

Calc

Program

System Data Word Agenda Time World Calc Program

happening. As you press the arrow key you are extending a black bar over the text – you are 'highlighting' it. You highlight text by moving the cursor while the Shift key is pressed. The highlighting starts at the original cursor position and ends where you like.

> To move or delete larger quantities of text, first you need to highlight it. This is very easy to do. It simply involves **holding down the Shift key** as you move the cursor with the arrow keys…

To delete or move larger quantities of text you have to highlight it. You do this by placing the cursor where you want to start the highlighting, then hold down the Shift key as you move the cursor to where you want the highlighting to end. Use the arrow keys as normal for this (including the Psion & Control combinations).

Be careful, though, because you can wipe out large chunks of text this way! For now, just highlight one word. OK? Now press Delete. Hey presto! – the whole word is gone.

Now for deleting just a few letters or characters, this method is no quicker than simply tapping the Delete key repeatedly. But for larger quantities of text it's a huge time-saver. Just remember, all you have to do to highlight text is to move the cursor to where you want to start, then use Shift with the various cursor control commands (arrow, Control+arrow, Psion+arrow) to move it to where you want the highlighting to end.

If you change your mind at any point, or you realise you've highlighted too much or the wrong text, you can put it right very easily just by moving the cursor back, 'unhighlighting' text as needed. Or you can cancel the whole operation by releasing the Shift key and pressing one of the arrow keys.

• **You delete text in a document for two reasons: either because you don't want it or because you want to replace it. If you want to replace it, you don't have to use the Delete key. Just highlight the text you want to replace and then start typing your new text. Or, if that's too confusing, Delete and then start typing –It doesn't make any difference.**

Cutting and pasting

Word processors are great for correcting mistakes before they're printed, but they're useful for much more than that. They will also let you *reorganise* your work before you print it. You can take chunks of text from one part and put them somewhere else, reordering your ideas as you gradually refine what you've written. This process is called 'cut & paste' – 'cutting' a piece from one part of a document and 'pasting' it down somewhere else.

You do this in Word on the Psion in much the same way as you delete text – i.e. by highlighting the desired text. This time, though, you don't necessarily delete it. You have two choices:

(a) Copy the text to another point in the document...

(b) or Move it to that point.

To Copy text to another point, first highlight, or 'select' the text, then press the Menu key, select the Edit menu, and then choose the Copy Text option. Press Enter to 'remember' the text. Now you can move the cursor to the point in the document where you want the copied text to be inserted.

• **Note that as soon as you use the arrow keys, the**

System

Data

Word

Agenda

Time

World

Calc

Program

75

System   Data   Word   Agenda   Time   World   Calc   Program

highlighting on the text disappears. Good, you want it to! Highlighting is cancelled the moment you move the cursor without the Shift key depressed.

Found the right spot? Good. Press the Menu key again, select the Edit menu and then the Insert Text option. When you press Enter, the copied text will be inserted at the cursor position.

What you've done here is to *duplicate* a section of text – the Copy command leaves the text originally highlighted where it was. If you want to *Move* a section of text, however, the prodecure is slightly different. Select the required text as before, but this time simply press Delete. Don't worry – you haven't lost your text! In fact, the Psion temporarily remembers everything you delete. It stores it in a 'buffer'. The contents of this buffer will only be lost when you switch the machine off or delete something else (at which point it remembers *that* instead).

OK. Now move the cursor to the point you want the text to be moved to. Choose the Insert Text option (just like you do when copying text) and your words will reappear at the cursor position.

• **When you're moving text don't delay in re-inserting it. The text being moved is only safe as long as you don't delete anything else before you re-insert it. If you *have to* delete something else before you insert your text, though, press Shift+Delete. This deletes text *without* saving it to the machine's buffer, therefore it doesn't wipe over your saved text.**

Printing

At this stage you're probably ready to start either printing documents out or transferring them to a full-size desktop computer. The Psion is perfectly capable of doing these things. You will need to buy the appropriate cable, however, and may need to alter one or two settings.

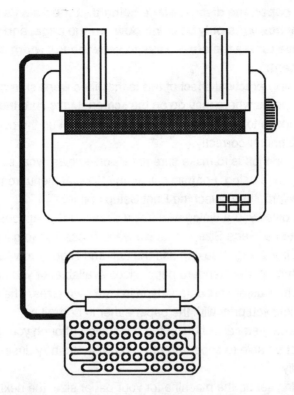

You can print out documents as easily with the Series 3 as with a full-size desktop machine. To find out how to link it up to a printer, turn to the chapter on Printing.

To find out exactly how to set up your Series 3 to 'talk' to either your own printer, or your own desktop machine, consult the relevant chapters in this book.

Although the Series 3 does a good job of showing you how your text will look on paper, the visible margins are decided by the screen size, not the margins set for printing.

• **You can 'preview' the layout of any document prior to printing by calling up the Word menu and selecting the Use Printer Layout option. This displays text exactly as it will**

System

Data

Word

Agenda

Time

World

Calc

Program

System   Data   Word   Agenda   Time   World   Calc   Program

fall on paper, the disadvantage being that the Psion's small display now acts only as a 'window' on the page, and you will have to use the arrow keys to view the full width of the document.

The only practical effect of this is that lines won't start and end on paper where they do on the screen. Make sure then, if you propose to print documents, that you've set up the page and the printer correctly.

Your first job is to make sure the Psion 'knows' what size paper you're using. For this, call up the Special menu from within Word, then select the Print Setup option.

This gives you a dialog with half a dozen further options. It's the first one, Page Size..., that we want. Press Tab to get the Page Size dialog. You can use the Left and Right arrow keys to cycle through the standard paper sizes available, or you can select the Custom option and type in your own sizes. The final option lets you print with the paper either in portrait or landscape (vertical or horizontal) orientation (though your printer may not be able to cope with anything wider than A4 inserted vertically).

Having set up the machine for your paper size, the next job is to set up the margins you require. (At the risk of stating the obvious, the margins are the clear strip between the edge of the paper and where any characters will be printed.) This is the second option from the top in the Print Setup dialog.

• **These dialogs are 'nested', one inside the other. To retrace your steps, just keep pressing Enter (to confirm your selection) or Esc (to retrace your steps).**

Press Tab with the Margins... option highlighted and you get the Margins dialog. You can adjust the Top, Left, Bottom and Right margins individually.

The rest of the options in the Print Setup dialog can be ignored for the moment.

What you've just done is set up the Psion to use a specific

size of paper and not to print outside specific boundaries (the margins) on that paper. These were printer settings. From now on, all we're going to be doing is changing the appearance and the layout of the text within this print area.

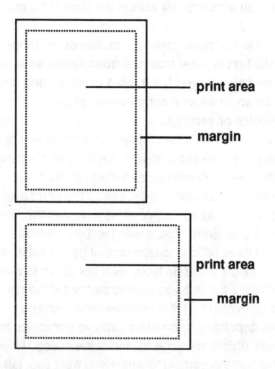

When you want to print, your first job is to set up the Psion with the paper size you want to use and the top, bottom, left and right margins. You can also print in vertical or horizontal form (many printers can't cope with paper wider than A4 inserted vertically, however).

You could just leave it at this. When you print out a document, the text will be laid out neatly enough. However, most people use Tabs to indent paragraphs, so let's see how you can set those up.

Tabs are a 'paragraph style'. Many of the styles you can apply with Word apply to whole paragraphs at a time. The next paragraph you write could have a whole new style. Or, if you end one paragraph and immediately start typing another, the new paragraph automatically adopts the style of the previous one.

• **Here, the word 'style' covers a multitude of things – whether the text is inset from the boundaries, what size it's to be printed at, whether it's in bold or italics and more. 'Style' is taken to mean a combination of text characteristics or settings.**

If you want to create a fairly simple-looking document, you will probably want the same style throughout. In this case, we'll assume the same Tab settings all the way through.

Before you write anything, then, call up the Word menu and select the Alter Paragraph option. This produces the Alter Paragraph dialog. From here, select the Tabs dialog.

There are three options to take care of here. First of all, you can set up to eight separate tabs, each one given its own number. Choose the one you want to set then move down to the next option – Position. This is given either in inches or millimetres, depending upon which units your machine has been set up to use (this is shown at the top of the dialog). Now change this figure according to where you want your tab stop to be. The third option governs the type of tab you want – Left, Centre or Right.

• **Remember that if several tabs have been set up, the last two settings – Position and Type – will change on-screen each time you change the Select Tab option. Each tab, from 1-8, has its own Position and Type settings.**

Now if you've done everything correctly, when you get back to your document and start typing, the Tab settings should be at exactly the position or positions you selected. Remember, though, that you're viewing a small display, and while a 6-inch tab may print out OK, it certainly won't display OK on a screen only 5 inches wide!

• **You may find that changing the tab setting appears not to have worked. When you've finished making changes in the Tab dialog, press Enter to leave it and return to the 'parent' Alter Paragraph dialog. Now you may be used to pressing Esc to get back to your document. DON'T. As far as the Psion is concerned, Esc means 'forget the settings just made' – and that includes any settings in sub-dialogs. Press Enter instead.**

What you see is what you get...

At this point we're going to throw in a new term – WYSIWYG (pronounced 'Wizzywig'). It's an acronym which stands for 'What You See Is What You Get'. The idea is that what you see on your computer's display should be exactly what you will get when your document is printed out. In this case, a 1-inch tab should appear as 1 inch wide on-screen.

As another example, if you underline certain words in your document, they should appear underlined on screen. If you set others in italics or bold, they should appear in italics or bold on-screen. Also, some programs will let you set text in different sizes. This too should be shown on-screen.

The ultimate example of a WYSIWYG system is 'desktop publishing' software. This lets designers construct magazine and newspaper pages on a screen, knowing that they will appear on paper exactly how they look.

This is less important for word processing purposes, but it's still useful to know what your work is going to look like before it's printed. And when you're revising and reading what you have written (or, especially, what someone else has written) on-screen, it's much better to have underlined and bold words *shown* as underlined and bold than surrounded by various weird heiroglyphics (until quite recently, most word processors

System

Data

Word

Agenda

Time

World

Calc

Program

Word

Most writers use *italics*. **bold text** and <u>underlining</u> to add emphasis to their words, where necessary. *The Psion Organiser 3 can display all three on-screen.*

The Word progam has a (partially) 'WYSIWYG' display ('What You See Is What You Get'). Bold, italic and underline text styles are shown on-screen as they will be printed.

couldn't show different text styles, and you had to insert special codes either side of the relevant text to get it to print out in the desired way).

The Series 3 goes a long way towards showing you what you're going to get when the document is printed. It doesn't offer a true WYSIWYG display – there are some things it simply *can't* show – but you still get a good idea.

Setting typestyles

For a start, you can set text in a variety of styles. Try highlighting a word or phrase, then, holding down the Control key, press BB – the text is now in bold. What's more, it shows up as bold on the screen. You can do the same thing when you want to italicise text, or underline it.

Word will also let you set text in superscript or subscript by the same method. However, these two styles are *not* shown on-screen, it would pose too many technical problems.

It doesn't stop there, though. Depending on the printer you're using, Word can also print text in different fonts (that is, different character styles) and different sizes. These aren't shown on-screen as they will be printed, but there are still ways of checking how your document will look before you print it, as we shall see later.

The styles you can apply, and the commands for applying them are:

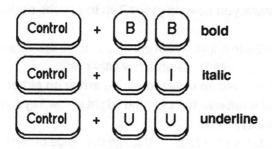

(shown on-screen)

Control + **S** **S** superscript

Control + **E** **E** subscript

(not shown on-screen)

The Alter Paragraph dialog

Most of the styling and layout changes you can make are accessed from our friend the Alter Paragraph dialog. Let's take a closer look at each of the six options within the dialog:

Font... When the dialog appears, the Font option will be highlighted. Unless it's already been tinkered with, it should be displaying the default setting – **Proportional 12**. This means that the font being used is 'proportional' (i.e. a narrow letter like 'i' takes up less space than a wide one like 'w') and that it will be

System

Data

Word

Agenda

Time

World

Calc

Program

System   Data   Word   Agenda   Time   World   Calc   Program

printed at a size of 12 'points' (One 'point' is 1/72" – it's a printing term).

You can experiment with these settings if you like. How? Press Tab.

• **When you see an option in a dialog followed by three dots, it means you have to press Tab to see the option in full.**

Now you'll see a fuller list of options, and the first one – Font – (already highlighted) has an arrow either side.

• **If an option has an outward-facing arrow on either side it means you must use the Left and Right arrow keys to view the choices available.**

Use the arrow keys to cycle through the range of choices available. Whether you can print these depends on your printer. The Series 3 is initially set up for the Canon BJ10e bubble-jet printer, but you can use most other models. Other machines may be less sophisticated, and offer fewer options. Anyway, these options are: Proportional, Pica, Elite (Pica and Elite are two standard 'typewriter' styles) and 'Inherited'. We won't worry about 'Inherited' just yet, but Pica and Elite are quite interesting, if only because they are non-proportional fonts. That is, each character, no matter what its actual size, takes up the same width of paper when printed… and when displayed. Choose either Pica and Elite and you will notice that your text now looks different, more spaced-out. That's because it's now being displayed non-proportionally.

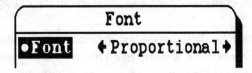

Many of the Series 3's dialogs contain items with an arrow either side. This is to indicate that there is a range of preset

options, and that you can cycle through them using the left/right arrow keys.

Size – If you select the size option you'll see a range of sizes on offer which you can cycle through with the Left and Right arrows. Remember, the Series 3 will be set up to work with a Canon BJ10e, so some of these sizes may not be available on your printer.

Underline, Bold, Italic – These can be set here, as well as with the special codes described earlier. However, if you try altering them you will get *three* options: On, Off and Inherited. This is best explained with an example. Imagine you have a paragraph of plain text, but with one word picked out in bold. Now you want to change that paragraph's font, so you call up the Font dialogue. However, if you leave the Bold setting in that dialogue On, *all* the words in the paragraph will be made bold. If you set it to Off, *none* of them will be in bold. The only way to keep that one word in bold is to set the Bold option to Inherited – the new paragraph will 'inherit' the previous paragraph's style setting.

Print position – This is a bit mysterious. The machine will dourly inform you that this 'cannot be changed' if you try to fiddle with it. In reality, it's not actually all that mysterious. It relates purely to subscript or superscript text. The Psion refuses to print entire paragraphs in subscript or superscript form!

Indents – This dialog lets you set up a left and right indent for a paragraph or series of paragraphs. This is nothing to do with the margins setting, since that applies to the whole document. Instead, the Indents command lets you indent some text relative to the rest .

Apart from left and right indents, you can also specify a First Line Indent. Hence you can have the first line of each paragraph *not* indented from the left at all. Or it can be indented further than the rest of the text. You can't specify a first line right indent.

Tabs – We've already covered Tabs above at some length, so

System

Data

Word

Agenda

Time

World

Calc

Program

there's no need to go into them again now.

Alignment – Do you want your text to have a ragged right edge (left-aligned)? Or do you want it aligned to the right? Or centred? Or justified (the words on each line spaced out so that both left and right edges are straight)?

You can set up any of these with this dialog. The Psion will show all of these alignments on-screen, except for the justified option, which it *can't* display (instead it's displayed as left-aligned text).

Spacing – We've looked at different fonts and different font sizes, but we haven't looked at line spacing yet. Typewriters usually offer you single spacing, 1/2 line spacing or double-spaced type, and the Series 3 offers you the same kind of control – more, in fact.

The Line Spacing in this dialog is displayed as 'points' (1/72nd of an inch). You may need to experiment to find the settings that suit you, but generally, you want line spacing slightly larger than the size of the text you are using. So if your text is 12 point, your line spacing should be 14.

Space Above relates to paragraph spacing. Do you want additional spaces between each paragraph? If so, you can add it here (set it to 14 for a whole line space for our example)...

...Or with the Space Below option. They both have the same effect, except that one adds the space at the top, one at the bottom.

- **It's up to you whether you use the Space Above/Below options. You can get much the same effect just by adding blank lines between paragraphs – and it's much easier to see what you've done. If you want all the paragraphs in a document spaced, though, it's probably worth using these options.**

Keep Together, Keep With Next and Start New Page are all related. They let you control how paragraphs are printed on the page. Specifically, they let you decide where page splits occur.

Keep Together, when set to Yes, prevents that paragraph from being split if it falls at the end of a page. If it won't fit on the bottom of a sheet, it's simply transferred whole to the start of the next.

Keep With Next stops a paragraph from being separated from the following one. If the next paragraph doesn't start until the next page, this one is taken across to the next page too. (This is actually quite useful as a style for cross-heads and sub-headings in text – there's nothing more useless than a cross-head on the last line of a page!)

Start New Page: when this is set to Yes, the paragraph is placed at the top of the next new page, irrespective of how much space was left on the old one.

• **None of the Spacing options are displayed on-screen when you go back to your text. You won't see the effect of changing the line spacing because the Psion's display is too small to make this practical. And you also won't be able to tell if paragraphs are set up to Keep Together, Keep with Next or Start New Page.**

Outline level   'Outlining' is a way of developing your ideas and the organisation of a piece of writing. It's designed to make it easier to view your piece at several levels of 'detail' – main headings alone, headings and introductions, or any other level you care to set it at. The point is that you should design your own outline according to your own needs.

More on this later, but for now… well, you know what it is, anyway.

Headers and footers
If you print out a report or the chapter of a book – anything that extends over several pages – you may want to put your name, page numbers or section-headings on each sheet. You do this with Headers and Footers. Headers go at the top of the page,

System

Data

Word

Agenda

Time

World

Calc

Program

Footers go at the bottom.

The headers and footers dialogs both work in the same way and contain the following settings:

Text This is what you want to be printed. It can be anything you like, but there are certain especially useful options, all prefixed by the '%' symbol:

%F   Prints the name of the file/document

%D   Prints the current date

%T   Prints the current time

%P   Prints the page number (another special character, **%M**, prints the *maximum* page number of that document, so you could specify as a header **%P of %M**, for example, which would print, "page 19 of 24")

%%   Prints a single "%" character – there may be times when you want to put this symbol in a header without the machine thinking it's a special command!

You can use any of the above as *part* of your header. For example, you could have **Today's Date is %D** as your header.

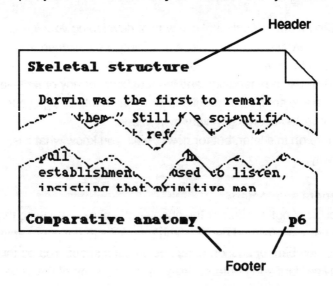

Header

Footer

System Data Word Agenda Time World Calc Program

Word lets you add 'Headers' and 'Footers' to the tops and bottoms of your printed pages respectively.

Alignment – Headers can be aligned just like ordinary text – but with a couple of extra frills:

Left – Standard left alignmen

Right – Standard right alignment

Centred – Standard centred alignment

Two column – You can print a header as two parts, say the page number and the date, separated by a tab.

Three column – As above, but for three pieces of information.

On First Page – If the first page of your document is a title page, or forms an introduction, or is in any way different from the rest, you may not want it to have a header. In which case, this option lets you 'switch it off' just for that page.

Font – The Font dialog looks just like the one in the Alter Paragraph dialog! It works the same way too, and lets you set the Header style independently of the text on the page.

Vertical Offset – How far above the main text do you want the Header to be printed? The distance is measured from the top of the Header text, so don't forget to include its height in the figure.

• **The Header and Footer dialogs are identical, and both work in the same way... except for the Vertical Offset. Don't include the height of the text when setting this for Footers – remember, the Vertical Offset is measured from the top of the text in both cases. Imagine both Footers and Headers as 'hanging' from their Vertical Offset positions...**

Handling Files

So far we've looked at how to create, edit and revise text on the Series 3. We haven't yet looked at how you store and retrieve it.

Throughout this section we've been referring to 'documents'. For 'document' you can also read 'file' ('document' makes more sense to non-computer buffs, but 'file' is the accepted computer

System

Data

Word

Agenda

Time

World

Calc

Program

89

term). Anything you write – be it a story, a report, a letter or whatever – is saved in the Psion's internal memory as a 'file'.

Now with most computers, as soon as you switch them off, whatever was in the machine's memory is lost – unless you've saved it either on to a floppy disk or on to an internal 'hard disk' (as fitted to most PCs these days). That's because computers use two types of memory: RAM (the computer's everyday 'workspace') and disks (permanent magnetic storage). You will work on documents using the RAM memory (because it's faster), but you must always remember to save your work periodically on to disk (because it's permanent).

The Psion is slightly different. Because it doesn't have an internal hard disk and can't accept floppy disks, all the information you type must be stored on RAM. Which means the batteries are always supplying a small amount of power to keep the contents of the RAM memory intact. No power = loss of memory!

• **The Series 3 has sockets for Psion's own 'solid state disks' (SSDs), which are basically RAM modules with their own battery back-up – essential if you mean to use several such disks and will be taking them out for storage.**

• **The Series 3 is very good at retaining data. Even if you take the main batteries out, the back-up battery, although not powerful enough to let you use the computer, will keep your data safe for up to a year!**

However, although your information is just as safe whether it's saved or not, you can generally only work on one file at a time. So to start a new file in Word, you first have to 'quit' or 'exit' the old one. And that involves 'saving' it into the Psion's own filing system.

To create a new file, call up the File menu and select the first option, New File. You'll see a dialog prompting you for a filename and some other information. For now we'll just worry about the filename. Choose a name, type it in, press Enter and you will duly be presented with a blank new document.

Now Word can only ever have one file 'open' at any one time. To open another file so that you can work on it, you first have to close, or 'exit' the one you're on. Let's say you've had enough of working on your new file – how do you get back to your old one?

(1) Call up the Special menu

(2) Select the Exit option (the last on the list)

(3) You're now back at the System screen. Underneath the icon for the Word program you will see a list of file names. Choose the one you want with the Up and Down arrow keys and press Enter

(4) You are now editing your chosen file!

or:

(1) Without exiting, press the System button below the display

(2) You will now see the same list of file names, but if you use the arrow keys you will see that the file you were working on stays in bold type. This means that it is still 'active'. Whenever you press the Word button you go straight into any active document. Select the file you want from the list

(3) The active file will be exited and the one you chose will be loaded up and will become the 'active' one

There are two other commands associated with saving: Save and Save As.

The **Save** command can be found on the Edit menu. What this does is let you save the file as it currently is. If you exit later on, that version is saved 'over' it. However, if you make some changes, then wish you hadn't (!) you can return to the previous saved version using the **Revert** command (also on the Edit

System

Data

Word

Agenda

Time

World

Calc

Program

menu). This is very useful when you're about to do something you're not sure about!

The Save As command is particularly useful for a number of reasons. For example, if you have prepared a shopping list for Tuesday evening and then decide you want another, very similar, list for Friday, you don't have to type it all out again. Simply write the list for Tuesday, save it as, say, "Tueshop", then immediately Save As "Frishop". You will now find yourself working on a brand new file called "Frishop" which you can adapt for Friday's shopping expedition.

Save As creates another copy of the file you're working on, but under a different name. It can also be useful when you're about to make major changes you're not too sure about – much like the Save and Revert option. However, this method doesn't involve making a choice between versions. You can keep them both.

The Psion has an efficient and easy-to-follow way of storing files. The files are listed on the System screen, under the program they were created with (in this case, Word).

However, the machine has only a limited amount of internal memory, and while it will take you a while to use it up, the time will come when you run out of space – time to throw some stuff out!

There is one golden rule here: **Use logical filenames**. What was no doubt a wonderfully witty name for a file six months ago will almost certainly be completely meaningless by now. And you don't want to have to go opening every file up to see what was in it before you can throw it away, do you?

Now Word lets you create documents, but it will also let you 'import' text and information. This information can come from three sources:

(1)   Other Word documents stored in the machine
(2)   The other programs provided with the Series 3

(3) Other computers

Word will let you Merge text from one document into another. To do this, first of all place the cursor at the point in your document where you want the merged text to start. Then call up the File menu and select Merge In. You'll now get a list of files to choose from.

• **The text merged in will bring with it its own set of styles and short-codes (see later). This is no problem – unless the codes are the same as ones already existing in the document you're merging into. If that's the case, the 'merged in' styles are overriden by the existing ones. It can get very confusing, and it might just be simpler to save the text you want to merge in as 'plain text' first (use the File Type option in the Save As dialog).**

To import text from one of the other Series 3 programs (or just a part of the text from another Word file), you use the Bring Text option on the Edit menu. Follow these steps:

(a) Open the file you want to copy **from**. To do this, press the System button, then select the file from the list below the appropriate program symbol.

For example, you might want to copy a name and address from a Data file. To do it, open the desired file containing the information and then highlight the text you want to copy with the Shift+arrow keys (you'll need to select the Update option on the Change menu)

(b) Press the System button again to return to the System screen. Now select the Word document you want to import the text **into**

(c) Move the cursor to the point in your document where you want the name and address to appear

(d) Select the Bring Text option on the Edit menu and hey presto – job done!

System

Data

Word

Agenda

Time

World

Calc

Program

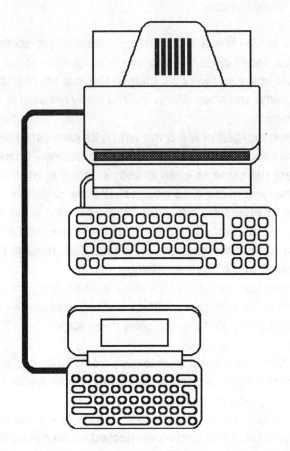

You can transfer text to and from full-size desktop machines, but for this you need the Serial-3 Link Lead, available from Psion.

Importing text from another machine is slightly more complicated. For this you need a special lead to connect the Series 3 to the other computer – The Serial-3 Link Lead.

A version of this is available for both PC-compatible machines and the Apple Macintosh.

- **For details on how to set up your Serial-3 Link Lead, turn to the appropriate section in this book.**

Depending on the desktop machine you're swapping text files with, you may have to convert your Word file to plain text. The word processing software you use on the desktop machine will probably be able to understand the normal Psion text files, but not the various styling and formatting codes they contain.

It's usually much easier to first save your documents as plain text. To do this, call up the Save As menu and choose a new file name (don't use the existing one, as you'll overwrite that file). Then change the bottom option, File Type, to "Text". Now press Enter to save your new, text-only, file.

Find & Replace

What if you've just got through a long business report, only to wonder exactly what you *did* say about your boss's management skills... and you've only got a few minutes to check?

Well rather than scroll through the whole document, you can use the Psion's Find Text facility. This command is found on the Scan menu, and it works very simply. You are asked for the text you wish to Search for, the direction you wish to search in (forwards from the current cursor position in the text or backwards) and, finally, whether you wish the search to be Case Sensitive. That is, if your boss's name is Don, you don't want the search to be stopping at every word with 'don' in it.

Case sensitivity can usually be left off, but there may be times when using it will speed things up.

OK, so you've found Don in the report, and you see that you've described him in glowing terms. That wasn't what you expected, and you're sure that *somewhere* you've stated a few home truths that you wish you hadn't... for this you need the Find Again option, directly below the Find Text option on the

System

Data

Word

Agenda

Time

World

Calc

Program

Scan menu.

Find Again doesn't offer you the chance to type in the text you want to find, since you already did that with the Find Text command. Instead, it just searches through your document for the *next* instance of the specific word (or part of a word).

Fine. But you may not actually have been rude about Don. You may instead have mis-spelt his name. Instead of 'Don', you've called him 'Ron'.

Well the Word software can also *replace* as well as *find* text. The Scan menu contains a Replace option. When you select this you get a dialog similar to the Find Text dialog, but with an additional option – Replace With.

As before, you can search forwards or backwards from the current cursor position, and you can set the search to be case sensitive or not.

• **The easiest way of remembering where a search is starting and finishing from is to make sure you return the cursor to the start of the document before you begin. Otherwise it's easy to lose track of which parts of the document you've searched.**

In use, the Replace function is quite different. As soon as it finds a match in the text for your chosen word or phrase it stops and offers you four choices:

(E)End   You abandon the search

(R)Replace   You change that instance of the text and set off to look for the next

(S)Skip   You leave that instance as it is, but set off to look for the next one

(A)All   You change this instance, and all the following ones automatically

This last option, All, is the most commonly-used and the most powerful. Make sure you really do want all instances of the specified text to be changed – it's easy to inadvertently specify what you think of as a whole word, only to realise later (when it's too late) that it also forms part of other words…

• **The Word software's Find and Replace functions can handle spaces, unlike some other commercial programs. Which means that if you are looking for all instances of the word 'an', for example (two letters which form part of many other words), you can search for [space]an[space]. This will find instances of an only when there is a space either side, i.e. when it is a single word and not part of another word.**

Styles

So far we've only looked at the different ways you can manually apply text styling. So if you wanted to indent a paragraph, for example, you would select the paragraph and then use the Alter Paragraph option on the Word menu to change it.

However, you can also set up specific styles for paragraphs which you can re-use again and again without having to go through all the rigmarole of specifying the indents, the tabs, the fonts, italicisation and so on.

In fact, every time you use the Alter Paragraph dialog to style a paragraph, you unwittingly create a new 'Style'.

You can also review and edit existing styles, some of which exist already as standard Word text styles. To do this, select the Styles option from the Word menu. You now get another series of options. Select the first, Review.

What you get now is a dialog which looks identical to the Alter Paragraph dialog. However, there is a difference. Now, right at the top, instead of the 'Alter Paragraph' title there is a line titled Style and a style name between two arrows. Remember, the two arrows indicate there are other options, so use the Left and Right arrow keys to see what they are. You should find **BT:Body text**, **HA:Header A**, **HB:Header B** and **BL:Bulleted**

System

Data

Word

Agenda

Time

World

Calc

Program

list. These four styles are all provided as standard. The two-letter code before the style name is a short-cut for applying them. Go back to the document you're working on, select a paragraph (you only have to place the cursor within it, not highlight the whole lot – styling changes only apply to whole paragraphs at a time anyway) then press Control+[two-letter code]. That style is then applied to your selected paragraph (you can style more than one paragraph at once simply by selecting more than one).

Apart from these four styles, you'll probably find some more if you've already been experimenting. These will have names like **ZA:ZA** and **ZB:ZB**. These are styles you have unwittingly created while you were experimenting with the Alter Paragraph dialog settings. You didn't give them a name, so the Series 3 gave them 'default' names. These always go ZA, ZB, ZC and so on.

If you intend to use the Word software extensively, you'll save yourself a lot of time and effort by producing your own styles, with names that will remind you what they do and short-codes that you'll find easy to remember.

To see how to create and edit your own styles, let's go back to the Styles option on the Word menu and see what the various sub-options do:

Review – This lets you examine all the styles currently in existence for that document. You can also edit them at will, making the same adjustments you would with the Alter Paragraph dialog.

Define – Here you get what appears to be the Alter Paragraph dialog again, but this time it's titled 'Define Style'. It works in just the same way, but at the end you are asked to specify your own name and your own short-code.

Apply – Presents you with a list of the available styles. You select the one you want with the arrow keys and then press Enter. This 'applies' the style to the paragraph currently containing the cursor (or any highlighted text if you want to style more than one paragraph).

Rename – If you don't like either the name of one of the styles, or the short-code it has, you can change them here.

Delete – Unwanted styles don't cause any real problems, but they do clutter up your document and make it take longer to sift through those available to find the style you want.

Find – This works in much the same way as the Find Text option, except that here you're looking for a particular *style*. You're given a list of those available to choose from, and then the software sets off to look for the next instance of that style. This may sound strange, but it can be very useful. For example, you may wish to go straight to the next section in a document – if this has a heading in a specific style, you can find it very quickly indeed.

Many styles will be obvious on-screen. The Series 3 can display underlined, bold and italic text, for a start, and paragraph indents and tabs will be clearly visible. There are style changes which won't be so obvious, however, and yet it can often be useful to know exactly what style has been applied to a paragraph.

You can, if you wish, elect to have each paragraph's style short-code displayed alongside it. This is called the Style Bar, and can be activated by calling up the Special menu, then selecting Set Preferences and switching Style Bar to 'on'. This reduces the available screen width slightly, but can be very useful when you are using a number of styles.

System

Data

Word

Agenda

Time

World

Calc

Program

Skeletal structure

exploding jellyfish off the
Maldives.
     Darwin's reaction to the
apparent combustibility| of the
indigenous wildlife was typically
phlegmatic.
     "If they wobbly beggars wants to

1

Skeletal structure

exploding jellyfish off the
Maldives.
     Darwin's reaction to the
apparent `combustibility` of the
indigenous wildlife was typically
phlegmatic.
     "If they wobbly beggars wants to

2

Styles are applied to whole paragraphs at a time. It doesn't matter whether the cursor is simply placed within the paragraph (1), a word within the paragraph is highlighted (2) or the whole paragraph is highlighted. Emphases are different. You don't get the same range of settings, but Emphases can be applied to highlighted text (2).

Emphases

Setting up a Style is all very well, but there is a drawback. You can only apply it to whole paragraphs at a time.

However, you can also set up Emphases (the option below Styles on the Word menu). A defined Emphasis works in much the same way as a Style – you define all the various settings you want it to have and then give it a name and a two-letter

100

short-code.

Emphases differ from Styles in two respects:

(1) They only allow you to define Font, Size, Underline, Bold, Italic and Print Position – not tabs, indents, alignment and so on.

(2) They apply only to highlighted text, NOT whole paragraphs.

When you come to Define a new Emphasis, you don't get the full Alter Paragraph dialog. Instead, you get just the Font sub-dialog. All the settings work as before.

• **On our machine we had trouble with 'inherited' settings. Basically, when we set bold, for example, to 'inherited', it didn't work – any bold text within the text highlighted was simply ignored and the new emphasis applied wholesale.**

There is one difference, however. Remember the mysterious 'Print Position' option right at the bottom? This can now be altered – you can choose subscript or superscript-style text. The reason we couldn't change it before is that we were accessing the Font sub-dialog from within the Alter Paragraph dialog each time – and you can't set entire paragraphs in superscript or subscript!

You find, change and delete Emphases in exactly the same way you do Styles. Select Emphases on the Word menu and you get a sub-menu containing the same list of options:

Review – Study/edit all the existing Emphases
Define – Create a new Emphasis from scratch
Apply – Apply an Emphasis to highlighted text (you're presented with the list) – works the same way as Control+[two-letter short-code].
Rename – Give an Emphasis a different name/short-code

System

Data

Word

Agenda

Time

World

Calc

Program

Delete – Delete an Emphasis entirely
Find – Find occurrences of specific Emphases within your document

Outlining

Outlining is a feature offered by a number of word processors. It lets you organise your ideas before you bash out your document in full. It also lets you examine a finished document at various levels of detail – displaying main headings only, main headings plus sub-headings and so on.

A full outliner will do far more than this, but the one built into Word is not terribly sophisticated. It may still prove useful, though. (At least you'll find out what that Outline option in the Alter Paragraph dialog is for...)

The principle is a pretty simple one. Each paragraph is given its own outline level – in the Psion's case, 1-9. Now the Word software has a special display mode where you can define how many levels you want to see. So if you go into Outline mode and select 1, only Outline Level 1 paragraphs will be displayed. You would use this level for just the main headlines. If you select to view at level 3, all paragraphs with Outline Levels of 3 **and above** will be displayed – i.e. level 3, paragraphs, level 2 and level 1 paragraphs. The same applies all the way down to level 9.

The advantage, especially on a machine with a display as small as the Series 3's, is that you can look at the broad structure of a document very much more easily.

• **You can also print Outlines. If you select the Print option while you are in Outline mode, the document will not be printed in full, but at the outline level you've set.**

Although this isn't its primary function, using the outliner can make moving around your document very much quicker! It's easier to find where you want to go, and it doesn't take so long to get there... just drop back into normal mode when you do.

102

System

Data

Word

Agenda

Time

World

Calc

Program

ORIGIN OF SPECIES
(preliminary synopsis)

Level 1 — **Frogs**
    With four legs
       I have seen these on
       my travels
    Other frogs
       Not sure about these
Big frogs
    Like you find abroad
       e.g. Wales
Level 2 ———— *Like you don't*
Hairy things
    Ones that bite
    Ones that run around
    Ones that make a racket
Wiggly things
    Slimy
Level 3 ———— Difficult to pick up
    Non-slimy
       Generally lots of legs

Outlining is an excellent way of organising your ideas. You give your main headings an outline level of 1, your sub-headings a level of 2 and so on, all the way down to your body text. Now you can view your document at different levels of detail by selecting an outline level to view at (e.g. choosing Level 3 will display Levels 1, 2 and 3).

When you first enter Word, you are in normal document-editing mode. To enter Outline mode, select the Outline option on the Special menu. You probably won't notice any difference! That's

System   Data   Word   Agenda   Time   World   Calc   Program

because unless you've been fiddling with the Outline option in the Alter Paragraph option, all your text will have been typed in at the lowest level – level 9.

- **The two headings styles already set up – Header A and Header B are set to outline levels 1 and 2 respectively.**

Start experimenting with headings and paragraphs, however, and you will see that in Outline mode, Word displays your document differently. Level 1 text is shown starting up against the left margin as usual, but lower levels of text are indented by increasing amounts – this makes it much easier to see how the organisation works.

Unfortunately, the Series 3 doesn't let you edit text in Outline mode. If you try, you are automatically dropped back into normal mode. The Outline mode is for viewing and printing only. A shame, because it could have been a great deal more powerful.

- **The 'quick' way of switching between normal mode and Outline mode is to press the Word button while you're already using the program. This switches you between the two modes.**

Although you can switch the Outline mode on and off with the Word button, you can only change the outline level displayed with the Outline option on the Special menu.

The Outline mode indents successively lower levels of text, making it easier to see how the document is put together. It's easier still if the different levels of text have different styles.

For example, main headings could be in bold and underlined, secondary headings could just be in bold, crossheads could be in underlined italics… and so on.

This not only makes it easier to follow the document in Outline mode, but in the normal editing mode too – which is probably more important, since you don't have the indentation to help you.

This is where Styles come in. The outline level forms part of the Style, so set them both at once. That way, when you write a heading, sub-heading, crosshead etc and give it your own heading Style you're giving it a specific outline level too. So that if or when you want to use Outline mode, all your text is automatically at the right level.

Word counts

Journalists, authors, scriptwriters... professional writers everywhere spend half their lives doing word counts. Almost all editors pay by the word, so you need to know how much you've written to know whether (a) it's the length you were supposed to produce and (b) how much you'll get paid!

You can do a word count in Word by calling up the Scan menu and selecting the Count option.

Even if you're not writing for publication, a word count can give you a good idea of how long/short your document is – a full page of A4, single-spaced, 12-point text is around 400 words.

Password protection

Worried that prying eyes might be looking at your Word documents? If you're in business you probably won't like the idea that someone else can read what you've written if you leave your machine on your desk. Fortunately, you can password-protect your Word documents individually.

If you don't want other people to be able to read your documents, you can give them passwords... make sure you don't forget the passwords, though!

System   Data   Word   Agenda   Time   World   Calc   Program

To do this, call up the Special menu and select the Password option. You are asked to Enter Password and then Confirmation.

- **Be careful! Once you have set the password and confirmed it, your document is totally protected. If you forget the password you will never be able to open that file again!**

If you decide you don't like the password you've set, all you have to do is select the Password option again and type in a new one – leave the line blank if you don't want to have a password at all. Remember, though, you have to know the old password to be able to open up the document and type in the new one...

- **Although passwords protect documents completely, these documents have to be closed. Until you either Exit a document (on the Special menu) or open up another document the one you've just this minute set a password for will remain open – and unprotected.**

Special characters

Word automatically starts new lines when the word you're typing is too long to fit on the end of the current one – automatic 'word wrap'. Usually you can leave it to get on with it, but there are special circumstances when you might want to interfere. For example, someone might have a double-barrelled name that you don't want split over two lines (you need a 'hard hyphen'). Or there may be a long word that you would like to be hyphenated at a certain point, but only if it falls at the end of a line (a 'soft hyphen'). Maybe you don't want someone's Christian name and surname separated (you need a 'non-break space', or perhaps you want to begin on a new line without starting a new paragraph – important for styling purposes (use a 'forced wrap').

The following commands do the trick:

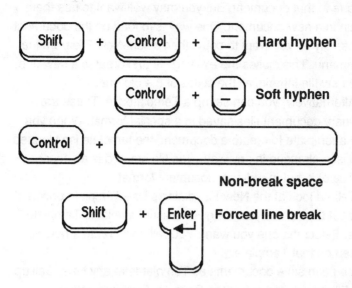

Shift + Control + ___ **Hard hyphen**

Control + ___ **Soft hyphen**

Control + _____ **Non-break space**

Shift + Enter **Forced line break**

As well as these, there are certain other characters that you use all the time which are usually invisible. All special characters can be displayed by first calling up the Special menu and then selecting Show As Symbols. This can be useful, if nothing else, for finding out why your document 'looks funny' or isn't formatted in the way you expected:

Tab displays as right arrow
Space displays as dot
Non-break space also displays as do (alas)
End of Paragraph displays as down/left right-angled arrow
Forced line break displays as down arrow
Soft hyphen displays as hyphen with a gap
Hard hyphen displayed slightly lower on the screen
at all times, not just when Show As Symbols is in use

Template files
When you set up a series of styles and emphases, these are

System

Data

Word

Agenda

Time

World

Calc

Program

System   Data   **Word**   Agenda   Time   World   Calc   Program

unique to that document. But you may well want to use them again in a new document. One way is to load up the document whose styles you want to copy, then select New File from the File menu. This closes the existing file and creates a new one. The new file inherits all the styles of the old one.

Alternatively, you can set up a Template file. These are ordinary document files saved in a special format. When you use a template to create a document, the template isn't loaded and isn't changed in any way – the file created is an exact replica of it, but in ordinary document format.

Take a look at the New File dialog's Use Template option. If you set this to Yes you are given a list of available Template files. Select the one you want. You will now create a new file based on that Template.

You can save documents as Templates at any time. Call up the File menu and select the Save As Template option.

Template files needn't be blank. They can contain text – for example, a letter template might contain "date" and "Dear…" on separate lines just to prompt you.

Evaluate

The Word software has a useful additional feature, in that you can perform simple calculations while you're writing. For example, type in "45/9", place the cursor anywhere within what you've just typed, select Evaluate from the Edit menu and the answer "=5" will be displayed!

You should leave no spaces between the characters in the calculation for this to work. If you do want to leave spaces you'll have to first highlight the calculation before you Evaluate it.

THE AGENDA

Do you have trouble getting your life in order? Too many meetings to attend, appointments to keep, jobs to see to…?

A diary is one solution. But it quickly gets dog-eared, filled with crossings-out and is generally inflexible – you only get so much space for each day. Worst of all, unless you're in the habit of checking it regularly, a diary can't *remind* you about that appointment with the boss that you're just about to miss!

The Psion Series 3's built-in Agenda software can do all this and more…

The Agenda program consists of three different 'modules'. The principal one is the Calendar. This gives you an overview of the current month (the left hand side of the display) and the current week (the right hand side). The week display will also indicate any appointments you've made.

If you press the Agenda button again you move to the Day screen. This is where you enter appointments and alarms

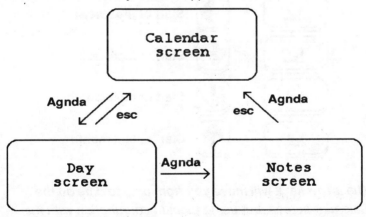

The Agenda program consists of three different displays – imagine them forming a triangle. The Agenda/Esc buttons move you from one display to another, as above.

System

Data

Word

Agenda

Time

World

Calc

Program

System

Data

Word

Agenda

Time

World

Calc

Program

Pressing the Agenda button a third time moves you to the Notes screen. Here you can store notes about jobs to be done on specific days, as well as a general 'To Do' list.

• If you're on either the Day screen or the Notes screen you can return to the Calendar screen by pressing Esc.

The Calendar Screen

The Calendar screen is really the nerve centre of the Agenda software. You use it to move to the days you want to make appointments/notes for and view the weeks ahead to see what's coming up.

Moving about the Calendar is easy. For a start, the cursor will be at the day you last inspected. To move it simply use the arrow keys. Too slow? To speed things up, press the Psion key while you use them. Psion+Left/Right arrow key moves you to the start/end of the week, Psion+Up/Down arrow moves you forward or back a month at a time.

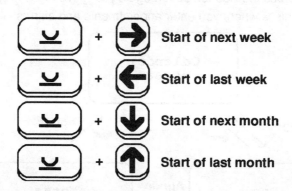

  ⊻ + ➡ **Start of next week**

  ⊻ + ⬅ **Start of last week**

  ⊻ + ⬇ **Start of next month**

  ⊻ + ⬆ **Start of last month**

The arrow keys will move you from date to date on the Calendar screen, but using them in conjunction with the Psion key will move you around much faster.

If all this is still a bit too slow for you (you may want a date a long way away from the current one) you can use the software's

Jump To Date option (on the Search menu). You just type in the day you want, press Enter and you go straight there.
• **If you want to get back to the current date at any time, just press Esc.**

The Day screen
You use the Day screen to set up appointments and alarms. First of all, though, you've got to get to the right day! The easiest way is to first move to the correct day on the Calendar screen, then press either the Agenda button or Enter.

The display is now given over to a single day, with the morning on one side and the afternoon/evening on the other. To enter an appointment use the Up and Down arrows to find the right time (use the Left and Right arrows to move between morning and afternoon/evening).
• **Don't worry that you appear to be able to enter appointments only at hourly intervals. This is just a guide. You can enter more specific times when you type in your appointment.**

When you've got to the time of day you want, press Enter. The cursor now changes to a flashing bar, indicating that you can now start typing…

Finished? Good. Now press Enter. You will get a dialog asking you for Start Time, Duration, End Time, Alarm? and Alarm Advance Time.

All of those are pretty self-explanatory. You only need to set two of the first three 'times' – For example, if you set Start Time and Duration, the End Time will come up automatically.
• **Note that you can't set appointments that run past midnight, the program won't let you. Curses!**

You then get to specify whether you want an alarm or not, and then all you have to do is decide how long before the appointment you want the alarm to go off.

Press Enter when you've made all your adjustments and you

System

Data

Word

Agenda

Time

World

Calc

Program

System   Data   Word   Agenda   Time   World   Calc   Program

will go back to the Day screen. The cursor has gone back to normal (think of it as being in 'browsing' mode), your appointment is displayed next to its time and, if you set an alarm, it will be accompanied by a little alarm symbol.

• **You'll have realised by now that it doesn't really matter what time you move the cursor to on the day screen - it's the time you type in yourself in the Appointment Details dialog that counts.**

The message or appointment description you want to leave can be pretty well as long as you like – it will wrap over on to new lines as necessary (three lines is just about the maximum you're allowed. Obviously, though, if you use over-long messages you're going to see less of the day on-screen. If part of your day *has* disappeared off the bottom of the screen, simply use the Down arrow to scroll the screen and bring it into view.

Appointments lasting longer than one hour are indicated slightly differently. The hours between the start and finish time are replaced by a vertical arrow.

• **It is possible to set up appointments which overlap (not very clever, though!). In this case a vertical bar is displayed instead of an arrow over the total time both appointments occupy. If you see this bar, start worrying!**

• **All these appointments you're making will appear on the Calendar screen (the 'week' view – right hand side). If you want to check, press Esc at any time – the week view part of the display will now have arrows indicating when you've made appointments. The length of the arrow indicates the length of the appointment.**

Although moving from date to date is quickest via the calendar screen, you can still move around quite freely within the Day screen. The Up and Down arrows move you forward and back one time 'slot' (one hour, generally) at a time, while the Left and Right arrows move you half a day at a time. In other words, from morning to afternoon to the morning of the next day and so on.

If you want to move faster than this, use Control+Left/Right arrow - this moves you a whole day at a time rather than just half a day. Psion+Left/Right arrow moves you a week at a time, while Control+Psion+Left/Right arrow moves you a whole month at a time.

Alternatively, you can use the Jump to Date option on the Search menu.

System

Data

Word

Agenda

Time

World

Calc

Program

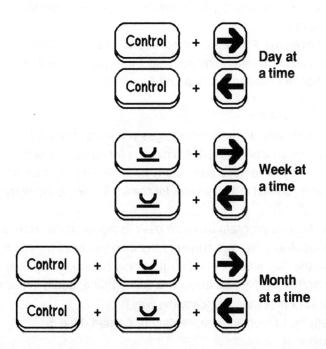

Day at a time

Week at a time

Month at a time

You can move about the Day screen faster by using the above Psion, Control and Arrow key combinations.

Alarms

The alarm system on the Series 3 is quite sophisticated. For a start, the machine won't let you set an alarm for an appointment

113

System   Data   Word   Agenda   Time   World   Calc   Program

on a date prior to 'today's' (makes sense). Plus you have the ability to set the length of time before your appointment that the alarm goes off. And when it does go off you can either press Esc immediately to cancel it, or press Space to silence it while you read the message.

And if you're not around to hear the alarm going off, the Series 3 doesn't give up! Instead, it carries on sounding at increasing intervals — every minute, for the first three minutes, then every hour four two hours. After than it doesn't ring any more, but it does display the alarm message when you first switch it on.

You even get a choice of alarm sound. Press the Time button, call up the Alarm menu, select the Sound option and then choose between Chimes and Rings.

Repeating entries

Some of the appointments/messages you want to leave for yourself will be one-offs. Others may be for items that occur regularly. If you've got a particularly bad memory you may want to remind yourself to leave work for the 5:15 train home every night!

The Agenda program makes it easy to repeat items. Here's how: first of all move the cursor to the item you want to repeat (still on the Day screen, don't forget). Now call up the Special menu and select Repeat Item. The dialog that appears lets you repeat your message the following ways:

• yearly (your wedding anniversary is a smart thing to remember...)

• monthly by date (for example the 22nd of each month)

• monthly by day (clever, this — the software stores the message on the second Tuesday of each month, for example, but links the week to the start of the month for a date in the first half and the end of the month for a date in the second half. So that, in our example, the last Tuesday in the month would be

just that — not necessarily the fourth.)
* weekly (straightforward enough)
* daily
* workdays (another neat option –if you set the alarm to wake you up in the morning to go to work, you don't want it going off at weekends!)

The Repeat Interval option is pretty self-explanatory. If you want an alarm to go off every three days, for example, you would set up a Daily repeat and a Repeat Interval of 3.

The Repeat From date is, by default, the date of the message you're setting up to repeat, but you can change it if you want to. The same applies to the Repeat To option — except that if you set Repeat Forever to "Yes" this line will be blank.

The Notes screen

As well as letting you store appointments and set alarms, the Agenda software also allows you to make notes. These can take two forms:
* Day notes apply to one day specifically. Different days will have different sets of notes
* To Do notes are the same as an 'Action List', or whatever executives are calling it this year. They are jobs you have to get done sooner or later, and you carry the list forward from one day to the next. You can also 'prioritise' jobs according to their importance.

Both Day Notes and To Do Notes are displayed on the Notes screen, and you get to this from the Calendar screen by pressing the Agenda button once (which takes you to the Day screen) and then pressing it again.

Day notes

The Notes screen is split into two parts. The top part is for Day Notes, and the bottom part is your To Do List.

System

Data

Word

Agenda

Time

World

Calc

Program

System Data Word Agenda Time World Calc Program

This part of the screen is for Day notes: they relate to specific days

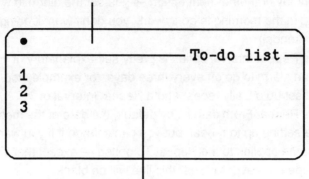

The bottom part of the screen is your To-do list. This is independent of the date and is carried forward from one day to the next

The Agenda's Notes screen is split into two parts. Make sure you know the difference between Day notes and To-do lists. And never try to carry out a 'Repeat Item' on a To-do list!

Entering a Day Note is easy. When the Notes screen is first displayed, the cursor is already positioned at the start of a blank line in the Day Notes section of the screen. Want to leave a note? Just start typing!

When you've written your note, press Enter. You will now be asked whether you want to set an alarm and, if so, how many days beforehand you want it to go off, and at what time during that day.

• **Using Day Notes with alarms is a very efficient way of reminding yourself of forthcoming appointments and occasions.**

You'll see that as soon as you've entered a Day Note another blank line appears beneath it. That's right, you can enter as many Day Notes as you like, each with its own alarm.

If you go back to the Day screen after you've entered a Day Note, you'll see that the note is displayed at the top of the screen as a handy reminder. (If you store more than one Day Note, it's the one at the top of the list that's displayed.)

To Do notes

You enter a To Do note in much the same way as you do a Day Note. The display, though, is a little different. There are three numbers 1, 2 and 3. Each of these numbers represents a different 'priority level'. Later on, when you get into the swing of things, you will probably have several notes against each of these numbers (depending on how busy/behind with your jobs you are!), but to begin with the lines are empty.

Try typing in a note. The procedure is much the same as making an entry on the Day screen or writing a Day Note: move the cursor to the line you want to write on and press Enter.

You are now in the editing mode, and can start typing. As before, when you've finished the note press Enter again. This time, however, instead of being given the option of setting an alarm, you are asked to set a Priority level. 1 is highest priority, 2 next highest and 3 lowest priority.

Now, when you press Enter again having made your choice, your note has been repositioned according to the priority you gave it.

When you have notes opposite each priority level, you enter further notes by moving the cursor to the very bottom of the screen, where there is always a blank line to type on. The procedure is the same — type your message, press Enter, choose a priority level and press Enter again to store your To Do note.

As with appointments and Day Notes, it's easy to edit an

System

Data

Word

Agenda

Time

World

Calc

Program

117

existing message. Move the cursor to the start of that line and press Enter. You can now edit the note. Press Enter when you've finished to store the new version.

It's easy to re-order jobs in your To Do list. To give a job a different priority, simply select it as above, but instead of editing it, press Enter – you get the Priority dialog again, which means you can set a new priority when you 're-store' the message.

You can also re-order jobs with the same priority. To bring a job to the top of the list, select it and then save it again straight away. The latest job saved with priority 2, for example, always goes to the top of the priority 2 list.

Editing entries

We've already looked at editing existing entries briefly. Here's how the whole editing process works.

The way you type in a new entry in either the Day Notes display, the To Do Notes section and also the Day Screen, is by first moving the cursor to the line at which you want to start typing and then pressing Enter. This puts you into the text editing mode. Only one menu is available in this mode – a shortened version of the Edit menu.

• **When you want to edit an existing entry you use the same principle – move the cursor to that entry, then press Enter. You will now be able to edit the message.**

The options you get are to Insert text, Copy text, Bring text or Evaluate. The first two options allow you to copy or move text from any of the sections in the Agenda to any other. So, for example, to move a Day Note on to your To Do list, move the cursor to the Day Note you want to move and press Delete. Now move to the bottom line of the To Do list section, press Enter as if about to type in a note and then select Insert Text from the Edit menu. Your note has now been moved!

Similarly, to move an entry from the To Do list to an appointment slot on the Day screen, move the cursor to the

System   Data   Word   Agenda   Time   World   Calc   Program

note, press Delete, move to the Day screen, press Enter at the time you want to make the appointment and select Insert Text again. Voila!

You can also *copy* messages and notes. This time, though you don't delete the original. Instead you must first copy the text by highlighting it with the Shift+arrow keys, then select Copy Text from the Edit menu. Then move to the place you want to insert the item, as before and use Insert Text on the same menu.

As with most of the other Series 3 applications, you can also Bring In text (the third option on the menu). For example, you might have an entry in a Data file that you want to use as a Day Note. Open up the Data file, highlight the required text, open up your Agenda file, place the cursor where you want the text to go, press Enter to go into the editing mode and then select Bring Text from the Edit menu.

The fourth item on this menu, Evaluate, can be found in the Word and Data software too. It lets you perform simple calculations while you're working. For example, if you type in "5+4" (no spaces) then place the cursor anywhere within that expression and Evaluate it, the machine displays the answer. If you do want to leave spaces, you'll have to highlight the whole calculation before you Evaluate it.

'Browsing' mode

When you're not editing or typing in entries, you simply be scanning the contents of your Agenda, or 'browsing'.

Three of the above actions — Insert, Copy and Bring — can also be found on the Edit menu in this, the normal (or 'browsing') mode, where you get the full set of menus. Trasnferring items this way is actually a lot quicker than pressing Enter to edit them first. However, in the browsing mode you can only move notes and messages wholesale – admittedly, this is all you will usually want to do – rather than

System

Data

Word

Agenda

Time

World

Calc

Program

119

parts of them. To transfer *parts* of messages you still have to go into the editing mode.

The other two options on the (full) Edit menu are Insert New and Modify Item. Select Insert New while you're in the To Do section, and it will put the cursor at the start of a blank line. Modify Item does the same thing as pressing Enter when you get to an entry you want to edit (i.e. it puts you in editing mode).

Searches

What if (horror of horrors!) you've forgotten the date of your job review? You know you made a note in the Agenda, but you don't know when!

Well you can find any Agenda item by first calling up the Search menu and selecting the Find option (phew!). The Find Item dialog lets you first define the text you're looking for (in much the same way as the Word and Data software will). It can be as small a 'search clue' as a part of a word, or as long as a phrase or short sentence (in practice, search clues never need to be very long). The search doesn't take any notice of capital letters, so your search clue can be all upper case, all lower case or a mixture of the two – the program will still find the same entries.

The next job is to decide what kind of entries you're looking for. You can search through either your Appointments or your Notes or both, but you'll speed up the search of you just specify one or the other. You'll also speed things up if you can eliminate Repeated Items from the search. One thing that the search will not include, however, is To Do notes (well, it's not too hard to simply take a look at those. After all, the list is independent of the date – there is only one To Do list).

Once you've chosen which areas to search, press Enter to start looking. The program will search 'forward' (i.e. into the future) until it finds a match. When it reaches the last day with an entry made in it, it will go right to the start of the file (the earliest date) and work forward from there to the current date.

When the program finds a matching entry, it will display the Day screen or Notes screen containing the entry, with the text itself highlighted. If it can't find a match, you'll see the message "Not Found". Grrr...

If you know that the entry you want to find occurs *before* the current date, you can search backwards too. Simply press Shift+Return when you leave the Find Item dialog.

Of course, it's one thing finding one instance of a particular word or phrase – but what if you know it comes up several times? Well once you've found the first instance, call up the Search menu again, but this time select Find Next. Or, if you're searching backwards, select Find Previous.

Files

Most people only keep one diary, but the Series 3 will let you keep as many as you like! Having too many Agenda files could get confusing, but you might want to have one file for the office and another one for home use.

To create another file, call up the File menu and select New File. Simply give the file a name, and there you are!

You can copy an existing Agenda file by calling up the File menu and selecting the Save As option. Simply choose a new name (no computer will tolerate two files with the same name – they get confused too!). You've now created an identical copy.

Agenda files can be deleted via the System screen. Make sure the Agenda program is highlighted, then select the Delete File option on the File menu. You'll be asked if you're sure (are you?), and if you select "Yes" the file will vanish for ever.

• **You can only delete closed files – those you have selected Exit from the Special menu while within the file.**

'Compressing' files

When you add information to your Agenda file, the file

System

Data

Word

Agenda

Time

World

Calc

Program

automatically grabs a little bit more of the Series 3's memory. If you delete an item, however, the Series 3 doesn't automatically grab that memory back. So that a frequently updated and edited Agenda file may take up a lot of memory, but may also be full of little 'holes' that could be reclaimed.

As you add information to your Agenda file, the file grows in size...

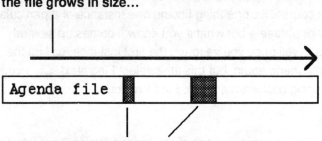

...but deleting information doesn't reduce the file size again. Instead, it just leaves 'gaps'

You will need to 'Compress' your Agenda files from time to time to free up unused memory – the Psion doesn't automatically 'reclaim' memory if you delete an Agenda item.

You can shrink or 'compress' Agenda files at any time by calling up the Special menu and selecting the Compress option. This makes the file smaller, releasing all the 'wasted' memory. You can do this with both Agenda and Data files, and it's handy when your machine runs out of memory. It's good practice to do it regularly anyway – say once a month.

'Tidying' files

Diaries (and Agenda files) are ephemeral things. Once they're past their 'read by' date, reminders, messages and notes are of no further use – but they still take up valuable memory space in your Series 3.

You can clear out your files with the Tidy option on the File menu. This deletes all entries made before a certain date. By default, the command suggests the current date when you go to use it, but you can define your own.

Ah, but are you a hoarder? Scared that there might be some gem of indispensible information lurking within those entries? If so, you can elect to save all the 'tidied' items as another, separate file.

Printing

It's one thing seeing all your Agenda entries, notes and messages on-screen, but many people still prefer good, old-fashioned paper. And you can indeed print out from the Agenda.

Details on how to set up a printer with your Series 3 can be found in the chapter on Printing, but to find out how to print out Agenda files specifically, read on...

First you need to call up the File menu, then select the Print option. If you want to print only a section of your Agenda file, then you need to define the 'From' and 'To' dates for the 'Range To Print'. Having done that, decide whether you want to print Appointments, Day Notes and To Do Notes, or any combination of those.

OK? Then all that's left to do is check that your printer is connected and on-line, and press Enter...

System

Data

Word

Agenda

Time

World

Calc

Program

123

PSION OF THE TIMES!

In these days of digital watches given free with every half gallon of petrol, it will come as no surprise to you that the Series 3 contains its own real-time clock. What do we mean by 'real-time'? Just that. The clock keeps time on a scale that you yourself respond to, rather than being based on some internal, and therefore completely useless, timescale (don't laugh. Until recently, many computers did just that!)

It will also come as no surprise that the clock provides alarm facilities, world time functions and all the other gimmicky time-based pyrotechnics associated with any far eastern LCD watch worth its salt.

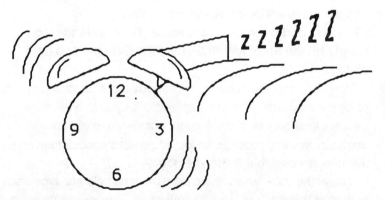

The Series 3 built-in clock provides full alarm facilities...

That said, the clock is exceptionally useful for anyone on the move, or for those with a social calendar slightly in advance of Howard Hughes's.

One of the clock's nicest features is its ability to display in both digital and *analog* modes. That is, as well as the usual digital readout associated with electronic timepieces, the Series 3 provides a very pretty LCD representation of a real clock face,

System

Data

Word

Agenda

Time

World

Calc

Program

125

complete with sweep second hand (known as 'analog'). You can feel at home with it right away, and of course being LCD, and therefore merely an illusion, there's no friction of moving parts and so it's just as accurate as the digital version.

Setting the time

Press the Time button. The screen clears and you're presented with the Time display. At the top of the screen the current date is shown. Beneath this, there's a box indicating any alarms which have been defined. At the right of the screen, there are digital and analog clock displays, and at the foot of the screen, your home city and country are displayed. The first alarm in the list is highlighted.

To set the time, summon the menu bar by pressing Menu. The Set menu will be displayed automatically.

• The first option on the Set menu is Time and Date, so simply hit the Enter key to display the Set time and date dialog.

You'll see that the Time field is already highlighted and that to enter the new time, all that's required is for you to type in the relevant information (say, 04 <right arrow> 25 <right arrow>, 00 <right arrow> and finally P, which would set the clock to twenty five minutes past four in the afternoon.

To set the date, arrow down from the time field and type each portion of the date (day, month and so on...) using the right arrow between each part.

Finally, press Enter to record the changes and set the new time and date.

• If you enter invalid information, the machine will simply display the maximum value in the range.

That is, if you enter say, 45 into the hours portion of the time field, 12 will be displayed.

Occasionally, the Series 3 will flash a little message on screen to let you know what has happened.

What time is it?

There's no need to switch into the Time application simply to see what the current time is. All you have to do is press Psion-Menu which summons a status window showing the time. Depending on what you're doing when you summon this status window, it can be made permanent by pressing *Control*-Menu (the Psion-Menu status window appears for a few seconds only).

Effects of the city...

Obviously, time being relative, the defined home city will effect the way the time relates to other World times on your machine. Different countries have adopted different base rates of time. Remember how you have to advance your watch by an hour after crossing the Channel? Likewise, the further you travel East or West, the more advanced or retarded will be the time relative to Greenwich meantime.

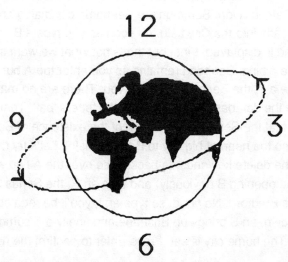

The Series 3 automatically adjusts to changing world time, enabling you to travel without fumbling with the clock...

System

Data

Word

Agenda

Time

World

Calc

Program

System   Data   Word   Agenda   Time   World   Calc   Program

Attempting to work out these time differences and correct the clock yourself would be tedious, so the Series 3 automatically sets the correct time relative to Greenwich Meantime if you change the home city. This is exceptionally useful if you regularly travel abroad. There's no need to mess around with the various clocks, just change the current home city.

To do that, ensure that you're currently in the Time application (and if you aren't, press the Time button now...), summon the menu bar by pressing Menu (the Set menu is automatically displayed) and select Home city. Alternatively, simply enter the Time application and press Psion-H.

• **When the Set home city dialog appears, the City field is already highlighted, so to set the city, start typing yours (or the most major city close to you) into the highlighted field.**

As you type, the Series 3 examines each keystroke and attempts to preempt you by displaying those cities which match your keystrokes from its database.

Here's an example. Let's say you live in the West Country city of Bath in Avon. Summon the Set home city dialog and start typing 'bath' into the City field. As soon as you type a B, Baghdad is displayed. Fine, but that's not what we want so continue typing. Baghdad remains as you enter the A but when you type a T, the Series 3 beeps at you. There are no matching cities in the database beginning with the letters 'bat'. That means that the Series 3 is unaware of the existence of Bath.

OK, so the nearest big city to Bath is Bristol. Let's try that. Press the delete key once, to backspace over the A (we want to keep the opening B obviously) and type an R, the Series 3 displays Bradford. No good, so type an I, you'll be regaled with Bridgetown, an S brings up Brisbane and finally a T summons Bristol. The home city is set. Press Enter to confirm the new city.

The time will change automatically to display the correct time for the new home city – whether this is a city in the United

Kingdom, or elsewhere in the world.

One thing. If you happen to live anywhere in Norfolk or Suffolk in the UK, as far as the Series 3 is concerned, you don't exist! No Norwich, no Great Yarmouth, no Ipswich, nothing! Probably doesn't matter on a world scale as far as time and distances are concerned, but rather an odd omission anyway...

In the summertime

Every country copes with summer time in a different way. In the UK, we advance and retard the time by an hour depending upon whether it's summer or winter.

In the UK, time is advanced or retarded by an hour during winter and summer respectively. The Series 3 performs these seasonal changes automatically.

You can effect the same operation from within the Time application of your Series 3. That is, you can switch the summertime control on and off for your home city and any of

System

Data

Word

Agenda

Time

World

Calc

Program

129

three zones: European, Northern and Southern. Obviously, if you change the summertime settings, some World times will be wrong, but that's what you pay for complete control over the system!

So. Let's say summertime has arrived, and you want to retard the clock by and hour. Enter the Time application and press Psion-S. When the Set summer times dialog is displayed, toggle the setting for you home city to 'on' using the arrow keys (you can also alter the three zones here too).

Toggle the summertime control to off using the same method when official wintertime arrives.

Workers' playtime

The Series 3 clock can also be programmed to take working days into account. Why? To enable alarms to be set to ring on work days only (you'll appreciate this after the first time you're woken at 6.30am on Sunday morning by an insistent pocket computer…).

To see a list of the current settings for work days and rest days, and to specify which days are your working days, move to the Time application and select Workdays from the Set menu, or press Psion-W. When the list of days is displayed, press Tab to see the current settings, or use the left and right arrow keys to move between the days on the list, assigning either an R (to signify rest day) or a W (for work day) to each of them.

Sound the alarm!

The Series 3 enables you to set up to four independent alarms, and each can ring once, once a week, every day or workdays. Each of the alarms is displayed on its own status line in the Time application.

To set an alarm, enter the Time application and use the arrow keys to select an alarm line currently displaying 'No alarm' (initially, none of the alarms are set), then press Enter. The Set alarm dialog is displayed and the Time field highlighted.

Enter a time (in either 12- or 24-hour format depending on what you've elected to display) using the arrow keys to move between hours and minutes. If you want to enter an hour in single figures, say, 2 for two o' clock, type a leading zero and the number (i.e. '02').

Arrow down to the Day field and choose a day either by typing one (the Series 3 preempts your typing by making guesses as each letter is entered) or by toggling through them with the left and right arrow keys.

Finally, arrow down to the Repeat field and enter or toggle 'once', 'daily', 'workdays' and so on on. Now press Enter to set the alarm.

Enter a number outside the permitted range and the maximum value in that range is displayed in its stead. If you set an alarm which falls before the current time (i.e. in the past…) the Series 3 sets that alarm to fall at the same time a week ahead.

After setting the alarm, the Series 3 displays a status line showing exactly when the next alarm will ring. This is very useful and saves you from worrying about whether you've actually set the thing up correctly or not!

To change an existing set alarm, highlight, press Enter and change the details displayed in the resulting Set alarm dialog.

The bells, the bells!
The Series 3 provides a choice of alarm sounds including a Westminster chime (just like Big Ben…) and an insistent electronic bleeping which frankly, is a pain (but then, that's exactly what an alarm should be to get you to respond, right?).

System

Data

Word

Agenda

Time

World

Calc

Program

131

System   Data   Word   Agenda   **Time**   World   Calc   Program

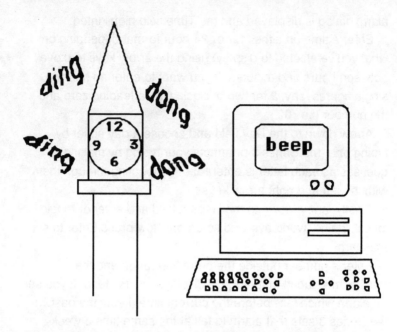

Chose between a Westminster chime and a computerish beep for your Series 3's alarm sound...

To choose an alarm sound, move to the Time application, summon the menu bar and, from the Alarm menu, select Sound (or press Psion-N on the Time screen). When the Alarm sounds dialog is displayed, select chimes or rings for both Time and Agenda alarms.

On being alarmed...
When an alarm rings, it takes over the Series 3 and won't allow you to do anything else with the machine until you've responded to its prompt via the alarm screen.

Similarly, if the machine was switched off when the alarm sounds, opening the lid will reveal the alarm screen showing the time the alarm was set to go off, and two buttons: Clear Alarm and Snooze.

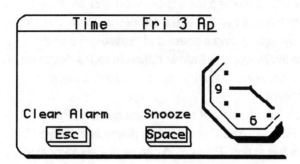

You won't be able to use the machine until you clear the alarm

Alarms ring every minute for the first three minutes, increasing the pauses between rings until the alarm rings hourly. If you still haven't responded to the alarm after the second hour, ringing stops, but you'll still be regaled with the alarm screen when next time the machine is powered up.

To switch off the alarm and continue processing, press the Clear Alarm button (Esc). Alternatively, you can temporarily cancel the alarm by pressing Space. This causes the alarm to go into sleep mode for five minutes – when the time is up, the alarm begins to ring again.

Snooze can be used repeatedly (i.e. adding another five minutes to the total snooze time each time) to a maximum of sixty minutes, whereupon snooze returns to five minutes.

A day off

Regular alarms, such as those which get you up in the morning for work, can be temporarily cancelled too (when you're taking a day off for example), without losing the alarm details.

To cancel an alarm temporarily, move to the Time application, highlight the alarm and press Psion-X (or summon the Alarm menu and select Disable...). A message flashes onto

System

Data

Word

Agenda

Time

World

Calc

Program

the screen confirming the cancellation and an 'X' appears in place of the bell symbol at the left of the alarm. Re-enable the alarm by highlighting it again and pressing Psion-X (alternatively, use the Enable option from the Alarm menu – Disable changes to enable when a disabled alarm is highlighted).

If you want to cancel an alarm altogether, highlight it, and press Psion-C. The Cancel alarm dialog is displayed for you to confirm the action. Press Y to cancel the alarm or N to leave it intact.

AROUND THE WORLD...

Where once the world was a place so large its vastness was outside the comprehension of mere mortals, now its four corners can be shrunk down, digitised and bunged into the silicon confines of a computer small enough to fit in your shirt pocket – and that's just what Psion did with its Series 3.

Inside your pocket pal, there are comprehensive details of the world's major cities, including displacement from Greenwich meantime, summertime factors, location, distance, and dialling code from your home city. There are more than 400 cities crammed into the machine so it's a rare occasion when you can't find the one you're looking for (unless you happen to live in Norfolk or Suffolk in the UK...).

Details of all of the World's major cities have been stored within the silicon confines of your Series 3...

System

Data

Word

Agenda

Time

World

Calc

Program

System   Data   Word   Agenda   Time   World   Calc   Program

You can obtain information about any of the cities stored in the Series 3, use the machine to tone dial a telephone number located within them, add new countries and cities or change the statistics associated with existing ones.

...in 80 days!
Or considerably less, if you decide to traverse the globe using the Series 3. Here's how to move around within the world application.

Switch the Series 3 on and press the World button. The screen display changes to a show familiar 2D representation of the world. There's a clock showing your home city's current date and time at the right of the display, and, if this is the first time you've accessed the application, the time and date of the first country (in alphabetical order) in the World database on the left of the screen. Below the map and clocks, there's status window with the name of a selected (not necessarily the *home...*) city and country, international dialling code and distance from the home city, and approximate sunset and sunrise times.

World

Use the World button to summon information about your home city and the rest of the planet

Let's say you're trying to call up Woody Allen who lives in Manhattan, New York (USA) to thank him for his latest movie, but you don't know what time it is there, and you don't want to be responsible for dragging him from his bed at some un-Godly hour of the morning. Not only that, but you can't decipher BT's international dialling code list, and so you need to discover Manhattan's dialling code too. A tall order? Not for the Series 3!

If it isn't already on screen, summon the World display by pressing the World button. Highlight the city field by moving to it with the arrow keys, and start typing Manhattan into the machine. As you type, the Series 3 examines each keystroke and tries to guess the desired city by searching it's database, displaying those which match your keystrokes – 'M': Madras, India, 'A': the same, 'N': Managua, Nicaragua ... and so on, until you try an H and the machine simply bleeps at you, stupidly!

What happened? Well, although Manhattan is a city with its own individual dialling code, it's actually part of New York City and must be accessed as such.

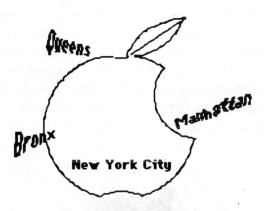

Cities are sometimes gathered together under collective titles...

So. Press Esc to return the flashing cursor to the start of the city field and type New York. When you reach the Y, New York Bronx is displayed. Fine, we've got New York, but we want Manhattan not Bronx, so now use the right arrow to cycle through the database alphabetically. First press brings up Brooklyn, and then with a second press, Manhattan is displayed.

The City clock on the left of the World screen changes to

System

Data

Word

Agenda

Time

World

Calc

Program

137

show the current time and date in Manhattan (actually in New York City...), and Manhattan's dialling code, distance from your home city and sunrise and set times are shown in the status window at the foot of the screen. You'll see that Manhattan is five hours behind the UK (if that's where your home city is) and so a home time before say, 2 o' clock, and it probably isn't advisable to call, but at least you've located the required information.

You can locate any city in the world (or at least, in the *Series 3* world...) using the methods explained above. Combine the arrow keys and typing strokes to improve efficiency.

You can also 'lock' the country, enabling you to cycle through only the *cities* associated with it. Choose the country whose cities you want to examine, summon the menu bar and, from the Edit menu, select Lock country. Alternatively, press Psion-L. The country is locked, and you can use the left and right arrow keys to cycle alphabetically through its cities. Pressing Esc, Enter, the up and down arrow keys or the world button itself unlocks the country (you can also unlock from the Edit menu...).

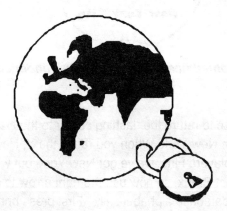

You can lock a country and cycle through only those cities associated with it...

What's the capital of...?
Just like finding a city, you can highlight and search for a country, and when it's found, the Series 3 displays its capital city (just think of all those 'what's the capital of?' general knowledge tests you're going to be able to solve easily now!).

To search for a country and its capital, move to the World application and use the arrow keys to highlight the country field in the status window at the foot of the screen. Type the country (the Series 3 will probably guess it before you finish typing), and its capital is displayed together with dialling information, distance from home city and so on.

Setting your home city
As well as being able to set your home city using the Time application, it's also possible to select it while you're within World. To set your home city, select a city using the city field and arrow keys as explained above, summon the menu bar and, from the Special menu, select Set home city (or press Psion-H). The Set home to 'CITY' dialog appears (where 'CITY' is the name of the selected city) for you to confirm the choice. Type Y for yes or N to leave the home city as is.

The lost city...
Not Atlantis, but a large part of the UK, as well as many possibly important (to you...) cities around the world have been omitted from the Series 3 – what can you expect? There's a finite amount of space in the machine, and Psion picked only those cities it felt to be important.

Unfortunately however, yours, or one that you're interested in might not appear in the World application. But fortunately, there *is* a solution. You can add new cities – even countries, and store them in a separate file in the internal RAM or on an SSD. There's limited space of course, enough for around 30 new cities, but that should cover the requirements of most of you.

System

Data

Word

Agenda

Time

World

Calc

Program

System Data Word Agenda Time World Calc Program

Here's how to add a new city.

Invoke the World application, summon the menu bar and select Add city from the Edit menu (alternatively, press Psion-A). The Add city dialog is displayed. You'll see a flashing cursor at the top of this dialog. Type in the name of the new city here. Next, down-arrow to the Country field and select the city's country. Continue to arrow-down, entering the city's longitude, latitude, dialling code, Greenwich Meantime offset and summertime zone.

What's that? You don't know what the city's latitude and longitude are? Nor its offset from Greenwich Meantime? Don't worry. There'll almost certainly be a city in the Series 3 World database which is close to, and shares the relevant data with the city you've just entered. Let's say, for example, that you want to add Bath, Avon (your home city) to the World application, but don't know what its latitude, longitude or GMT offset is. First, ensure that Bristol, a city approximately ten miles away from Bath, and one which *is* included in the Series 3, is on display in World's city/country fields, *before* you select Add city.

Now when the Add city dialog appears, you can 'borrow' Bristol's information (which is exactly the same) for Bath. Press Psion-A and type Bath into the Add city dialog. Remember to add the new dialling code, in this case, 225 (there's no need to enter the preceding 0), into the Dial code field, but leave all the other information alone. Now press Enter. You'll be prompted to position the map's cross-hairs over the approximate location of the new city, then press Enter again when the cross-hairs are in position. And that's it, the city is added.

• **Hold down the Control while using the arrow keys to traverse large distances in one move**

New cities are stored in a file called 'World' on the internal disk, although you can specify that further changes are added to a new file with a name of your choice using the New option on the File menu (World>File>New or World, Psion-N). To open one of

140

these files, select the Open option from the File menu or press Psion-O in the World application. These new city/country information files appear under the World icon on the system screen (rather like Word's text files...).

Country to country

It's also perfectly possible to add a country (although strictly, countries aren't added, but adapted from existing countries). The Series 3 has a finite amount of space for countries, and it has already been used. To add a new country then, you choose one which is unlikely to figure in your life. Somewhere you have no intention of visiting or working, a country where you don't have any relatives or friends. Next, select a country with a location close to that you want to add, and note down its summertime zone, GMT offset and so on (or else consult an atlas at your local library...), then select Update country from the World Edit menu and enter the new country's name into the Update dialog.

Remember to change the capital, national and international dialling codes (dialling country to country from without and within the UK respectively), and enter the previously noted summertime and GMT information. Finally, press Enter (...and be prepared for a longish pause as the Series 3 updates it's country database!).

System

Data

Word

Agenda

Time

World

Calc

Program

NUMBER CRUNCHING!

In keeping with most of the electronic gadgets available today, the Psion Series 3 offers a pocket calculator mode which you can use to compute day-to-day calculations such as shopping bills, racing certainties and the like. Unlike many of these other pocket calculators however, the Series 3 combines its abilities as a computer with those of the calculator mode to provide number crunching on a scale unavailable even with the most complex 'scientific' pocket calculators.

The Series 3 is perfectly at home with the most complex scientific calculations, as well as tracking your personal and business life!

Ten user-definable 'memories' are provided, and each can be assigned a meaningful name. In addition, there's access to the Series 3's OPL programming language so that you can use custom-written functions from within the calculator.

There's also a continuous 'list' of your calculator entries which is analogous to calculators with paper rolls attached. Unlike the paper roll machines however, you can scroll through the Series 3's electronic list and copy entries into new calculations. This is an extremely useful function which, used in conjunction with the memories, is very powerful.

System

Data

Word

Agenda

Time

World

Calc

Program

143

System Data Word Agenda Time World **Calc** Program

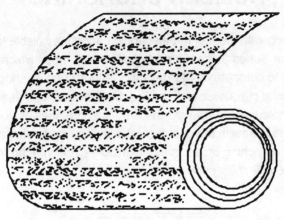

The Series 3 calculator maintains an electronic version of the paper tape which you can 'rewind' in order to review calculations...

Summoning the calculator

Switch the Series 3 on and press the Calc button. The screen changes to show a permanent clock in the bottom right corner and a calculator indicator to show that you're currently in calculator mode.

The main part if the screen is mostly blank. There's a dotted line across the lower section, the word Calc: beneath it and a flashing cursor. This is where you enter the figures, parentheses and so on which compose your calculations. Currently, there are no user-definable memories in use and the machine displays M1=0 at the top of the screen (meaning that memory number 1 is zero).

For those of you with large quantities of figures to type, the calculator can be made to display figures double-height, significantly increasing the clarity of the display.

To switch the machine into double-height mode, press Psion-B when in calculator mode. Switch back again using the same

144

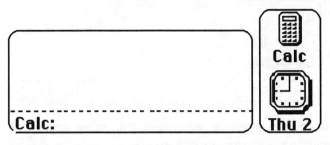

The Calculator main screen. There's a constant time and date read-out at the right-hand side

key-combination. Alternatively, press the Calc button while in calculator mode – the result is double-height characters (pressing it a second time toggles the display back again...).

Your first calculation

The arithmetic operators, +, -, * (multiply) and / (divide) are grouped together at the right-hand side of the keyboard next to the Delete and Enter keys. To obtain the results of a calculation, you can press either the = key (Shift-+) or Enter key. Obviously, the latter is far more convenient – there's no need to use the shift key, and Enter is larger and more accessible.

To perform a calculation then, switch to the calculator and start typing. Enter say, 2+2 then press Enter. The scrolling list (immediately above the dotted line) shows 2+2.

Below the dotted line, an equals sign is displayed together with the result of the sum, highlighted, followed by a flashing cursor.

Precedence

Like every computer, the Psion Series 3 performs calculations in order of precedence. That is, multiply and divide are performed before addition and subtraction. Here's an example.

System

Data

Word

Agenda

Time

World

Calc

Program

As each calculation is performed, it appears above the dotted line, with the result beneath...

Say you wanted to calculate:

15-12/3

If calculation was performed from left to right, the result would be 1 (15 minus 12 is 3, divided by 3 is 1). But because the division has a higher order of precedence than the subtraction, the result of the calculation is in fact, 11 (12 divided by 3 is 4, 15 minus 4 is 11).

To perform the calculation from left to right (i.e. to increase the order of precedence of the subtraction) you can use parentheses thus:

(15-12)/3

Now 15 minus 12 is worked out first and the result divided by 3 to give 1. Here's the order of precedence for the Series 3's arithmetic operators (from highest to lowest):

** (i.e. raise to the power of as in 2**4=16)
- (i.e. make minus as in -10+15=5)
* and /
+ and -

What this all translates to is that you cannot perform running calculations on the Series 3 as you can on a pocket calculator. With the latter, for example, you could enter a calculation such as 5+5-3+10*4 press equals and receive the result 68. That is, each number and operator is typed into the calculator in the sequence shown and the equals pressed only at the end to give the result. Each calculation, 5 plus 5, minus 3, plus 10 ... and so on is performed as it's typed into the pocket calculator.

If you did that on the Series 3 however, you'd get the answer 47 because the '10 multiplied by 4' bit would be performed before the additions and subtraction.

To get the Series 3 to behave like a pocket calculator, you'd have to press equals or the Enter key after each part of the calculation, or use parentheses.

Sticky fingers!
The Series 3 calculator features full error checking when in calculator mode. Hit the wrong key while typing a calculation, entering say, 5L4 (i.e. pressing the L key instead of the * key to its right) for example, and you'll be regaled with 'Syntax error' and the Series 3 positions the flashing cursor over the element in your equation it has detected as the syntax error – in the above case, the character L. Correct the error using the Delete key and type in a correction.

Another error message you'll encounter frequently is 'Unexpected name' – which indicates that the Series 3 has been told to use a function it doesn't recognise.

The electronic paper roll
Each time a calculation is performed, you'll see its component parts displayed at the bottom of the scrolling list above the dotted line. The calculator screen is capable of displaying the last five calculations, although a list of up to twenty calculations is retained and you can scroll this list to and fro using the arrow

System Data Word Agenda Time World Calc Program

System   Data   Word   Agenda   Time   World   Calc   Program

keys. Alternatively, you can scroll up and down a page at a time using the Psion key and the up and down arrows respectively.

• To simplify the calculator process, it's possible to copy calculations from the list and use them in new calculations. Use the up and down arrow keys until the calculation you want to copy is highlighted in the scrolling list (obviously you'll need to press the up arrow key first to move the cursor above dotted line and onto the list).

When the desired calculation is highlighted, press Enter. The calculation is copied to the right of the current cursor position below the dotted line.

Alternatively, if the result of a calculation is currently highlighted below the dotted line, it is *replaced* by the copied calculation.

Functions and percentages

The Series 3 calculator is equipped with a collection of pre-defined trigonometric functions, logarithms and powers, and you can also perform percentage calculations using the symbol provided on the 5 key (i.e. Shift-5). Let's look at percentages first.

To determine a percentage, enter the equation like this...

100*15%

and press Enter. The Series 3 displays the result 15. That is, 15 per cent of 100 is 15.

It's also possible to perform addition and subtraction while calculating percentages. Type this:

100+15%

and press Enter. The result, 115, is displayed. You instructed the Series 3 to add 15 per cent of 100 to 100. Similarly, to subtract 15 per cent from 100, type:

100-15%

and press Enter. The result 85 is displayed.

Now the fun begins. What happens if you want to determine what number a figure is a percentage of? Let's demonstrate. Type

75/15%

and press Enter. The Series 3 displays 500. What you've asked for is what number is 75 15 per cent of? Here are a couple of other interesting (and useful!) percentage calculations...

130>17.5%

Will give you 110.64 (i.e. £130 consists of £110.63 plus 17.5 VAT). This is extremely useful for those running VAT-registered businesses who are undergoing the quarterly nightmare known as the VAT statement. The function enables you to determine the net of a gross figure i.e. what a figure was *before* VAT was added.

Similarly, entering:

130<17.5%

will give you 19.36 - the amount of *VAT* of a gross price.

To make use of the Series 3 built-in trig and log functions, enter calculator mode and summon the menu bar by pressing Menu. All the functions, sin, cos, tan and so on have associated hot-key sequences so you can insert them quickly into a calculation.

When you select a function from the menu bar or summon it with a key-combination, the Series 3 displays it complete with parentheses at the current cursor position. The cursor is moved between the parentheses so that you can type a value for the function.

Alternatively, and with a result already highlighted, selecting a function displays it with the highlighted result automatically inserted between the parentheses.

Elephantine!

As well as the memory-type facility provided by the electronic paper tape, the Series 3 calculator provides ten user-definable memories. Each can be assigned a meaningful name and used to store intermediate results and other figures that you want to use later.

M1 is the default memory. You assign values and generally manipulate memories using highlighted results below the calculator's dotted line and the Memories menu available from the menu bar.

Each memory-oriented function, M In, M+, M- and so on has an associated hot-key combination which is far easier to use than accessing the menu bar every time you want to manipulate a memory.

Assigning a value to a memory

To assign the value 45 say, to the default memory M1, type the figure, then press Psion-I (alternatively, and with time to waste, summon the menu bar by pressing M1, and select M in from the Memories menu).

You'll see that where previously M1=0 was shown, the display changes to M1=45. This value remains intact until it is cleared by you, or manipulated in some other way such as being added to an intermediate result.

Manipulating the memories

If you've ever used a pocket calculator (and who hasn't?), you'll know that values stored in its memory can be added to and

150

*An elephant never forgets... and neither does the Series 3
calculator, with ten fully user-definable memories.*

System
Data
Word
Agenda
Time
World
Calc
Program

subtracted from intermediate calculations. Series 3 memories
are no exception.

You might, for example, calculate the VAT on an item sold by
your business by assigning .175 to M1 (type .175 into the

151

calculator, then press Psion-I). Now when you want to
determine VAT say, on an item worth £45, simply enter the
equation

45*m1

(i.e. 45 multiplied by memory 1) and press Enter. The result
7.875 is displayed – the VAT on £45.

Better still, you can assign meaningful names to memories.
Summon the menu bar and select Change memories from the
Memories menu (or press Psion-M). The Change memories
dialog is displayed. Down arrow to the New memory name field,
and type VAT. Now press Enter. Memory M1 is renamed to
'VAT'.

Now when you perform the VAT calculation on an item, type
VAT rather than M1. For example, with an item worth say, £23,
type

23*vat

and press enter. The VAT, 4.025, is displayed as the result.

As mentioned, you can add and subtract intermediate
calculations from the value stored in a memory. To do that,
simply press Psion and + to add the result to the memory, or
Psion and - to subtract it from the memory value.

In addition, you can use any memory name in place of a
figure in an equation. For example

10*M1
(45-23)/M4
1/4*1/2+M2

are all valid equations involving the values represented by
memories 1, 2 and 4.

More memories

The Series 3 offers ten entirely individual memories numbered 0 to 9. The default is number 1, but you can assign values to any of the others or choose one of them as the default working memory.

To switch between the memories, summon the Change memories dialog by selecting the option from the Memories menu or pressing Psion-M. When the dialog is displayed, arrow down to the Current working memory field and use the left and right arrow keys to cycle through those available. Finally, press Enter to fix your changes.

Back on the calculator screen, M+, M- and so on will now work with the newly-assigned working memory.

System

Data

Word

Agenda

Time

World

Calc

Program

PROGRAMMING

System

Data

Word

Agenda

Time

World

Calc

Program

The Psion Series 3 has a whole range of built-in programs designed to meet the needs of as many people as possible.

However, some users will have certain, specific, requirements the machine doesn't cater for directly. For example, if you spend a long time on the telephone each day, you may need to 'log' your calls – who you spoke to, the duration of the call, the outcome and so on.

None of the built-in programs can do this for you, but why not write your own program? The Series 3 has a programming language – OPL – built-in.

First of all, though, you need to know a bit about programming. Readers who know what programming involves already may just as well skip the rest of this chapter and get stuck into the Programming Manual that came with their Series 3s. We don't have the space here to teach you how to program your Psion. We do have space, though, to explain to beginners how computers operate and how you tell them what to do...

What is a program?

Computers are a complex system of chips and circuitry which, in a broad sense, works like the human brain. The central processor (like our brain) takes information from the machine's memory, it's keyboard or any other input device (like we take information from our memories and/or our senses). The computer then processes it to provide conclusions which can be displayed on-screen, printed out or translated into some other action. Humans 'think' in the same way to drive a car, answer a question or make a decision.

However, unlike a human brain, a computer has to be told what to do every step of the way.

Now since a computer is just a bundle of chips, wires and

155

System   Data   Word   Agenda   Time   World   Calc

printed circuit boards, we can't tell it in the kind of language we use. The language a computer understands is called 'machine code'.

Experienced programmers can understand and manipulate machine code. And because it's the most direct way to issue commands to the machine, programs written in machine code are fast and efficient – the computer will 'think' faster.

However, machine code is hard to learn and difficult to follow. Which is why other programming 'languages' exist. The best known is BASIC (Beginners All-purpose Symbolic Instruction Code). This is what's known as an 'interpreted' language. It is itself a program, and one that acts as a go-between for programmers and computers. The commands and language used when you program in BASIC are easier for us to understand and make sense of. And once typed in, they are converted into a form that the *computer* can make sense of. Using the BASIC programming language does have problems though, the principal one being that the interpreting process makes the resulting program slower in operation.

The Psion Series 3's OPL language is similar to BASIC. It's not quite as easy to understand as BASIC, but then it's a little faster and more efficient. And it's simple enough for non-programmers to learn, given time, so that they can produce their own programs.

Why should you want to program?

But why *should* you want to write programs for your Series 3? Well, there's the call-logging example above, to start with. The Series 3 is a versatile machine, but it can't be everything to everybody. The functions and programs most people need are included, but the designers couldn't allow for everyone.

Let's take another example. Suppose you are keeping track of your household expenditure. Your system is that you note down how much you spend and what you spend it on on a daily

Program

basis. Then at the end of the month you sit down and categorise the expenditure (shopping/petrol/bills and so on) so that you can arrive at totals for the month.

Well there's no built-in program to enable you to do this, but you can write one using OPL. The finished program could (1) ask you the amount, (2) ask you the category, (3) add it to a sub-total in that category, (4) total up and display the expenditure in each category when you've finished.

Programs like this are simple enough to write once you understand OPL and, via the Applications functions on the System screen, can be installed and run just like any other built-in program.

But we're not going to tell you *how* to program here. That would take an entire book; the *Psion Series 3 Programming Manual*, in fact. If you want to program your machine, roll up your sleeves and get stuck into that.

How long will it take to learn/do?
"Yes, but I'm a busy executive, I haven't time to learn programming!"

No, probably not. If you know nothing about programming, it could take weeks, working on it a couple of hours a day, to get to grips with OPL. If you know how to program in BASIC, it could still be weeks before you can turn out programs that are genuinely useful.

In fact, we think OPL is only useful if (a) you're a bit of a hobbyist and like tinkering about or (b) you really do *need* a specific function, and it's worth your while sitting down to program it. If your lifestyle is so busy that you really do need the organising power of the Series 3, it's probably going to be too busy to let you learn how to program… sorry!

System

Data

Word

Agenda

Time

World

Calc

Program

PRINTING

Typing in and storing information is one thing, but what if you want a hard copy of a Word file, or a print-out of a database? The Psion can print out documents using a wide variety of printers, via the appropriate cable. You will, however, need to set the Series 3 up according to the model you propose to use. This will usually prove extremely straightforward, depending on the model.

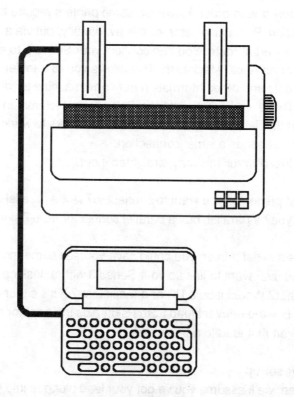

The Series 3 is initially set up to print via the Canon BJ10e bubble jet model, but it can also connect to just about any other printer on the market.

The Series 3 is supplied already set up for a particular printer – the Canon BJ10e bubble-jet. This is a very compact machine that nevertheless produces high-quality output and a wide range of type styles and sizes. However, you won't want to go to the expense of this model (it'll cost about twice as much as your Series 3) if you already have access to another printer.

Parallel or serial?

To begin with, you will need a lead to connect the Series 3 to the printer. Most printers need a *parallel printer lead*, and Psion will supply one to order. However, some printers require a *serial connection*. Psion also cater for this eventuality, but via a slightly different route. You can connect your Series 3 to either an PC or an Apple Macintosh. This allows you to transfer documents and other information from one machine to the other. These work via *serial links*. Psion manufactures an adaptor that lets you use one of these serial links to work a printer that needs a serial connection.

Confused? Well this may straighten it out:

1) What printer do you want to connect to? Is it a parallel or a serial type? If parallel, buy a parallel connector from Psion.

2) If it's a serial printer, you could save yourself some money. Will you ever want to link up your Series 3 with a desktop computer? Would it be a PC or a Macintosh? If it's either one of those, buy the relevant lead from Psion *plus* the adaptor needed to convert that lead to a printer lead.

Printer set-up

OK then, we'll assume you've got your lead plugged into your Series 3 (it goes in the expansion socket on the left-hand side of the machine). Now we have to make sure the machine is set up to work the printer properly.

To do this, press the System button This takes you back to the Series 3's 'nerve centre' from where all the major operations start (think of all the individual programs as 'branching off' from the System screen).

Now press the Menu key and use the Left and Right arrow keys to select the Special menu (far right). Now use the Down arrow to get to Printer Setup, and press Enter.

The dialog that comes up on-screen looks complicated, doesn't it? Well don't worry about it, because if you're connecting up with a parallel printer and the Printer Device option is showing 'Parallel' (the default setting) you don't have to do another thing! Just press Enter to confirm the existing settings.

If you want to use a serial printer, it's a bit more complicated. Press the Left/Right arrow keys a couple of times while on the Printer Device option and you will see there are two more choices for Printer Device: Serial and File.

Don't worry about File for the moment, that comes later. Serial is the setting you want.

Now your Series 3 should work with most serial printers on the market, but you may experience problems in some cases. If so, there's nothing for it but to study the printer manual and, if necessary, adjust the Serial Characteristics and Serial Handshaking settings.

You'll probably end up burning pints of midnight oil if you get too embroiled in this, but here is a brief explanation of what all the terms mean:

Baud rate
The speed at which data is transferred. The Series 3 has to send it at the same speed the printer expects to receive it! There are half a dozen standard speeds to choose from, but 9600 is the most common.

Data bits

The size of the 'packets' information is sent in. This is set either to 7 or 8. Again, both the Psion and the printer must be set to the same figure – and it will probably be easier to adjust the Psion rather than the printer.

Stop bits

Stop bits are a way of ensuring that the information has been transmitted correctly. Make sure both the Psion and the printer are set to the same figure.

Parity

A way of checking information has been transmitted correctly. Parity may be Odd, Even or None.

Handshaking

Amongst other things, this is a mechanism for letting the receiving device (the printer) tell the sending device (the computer) that it's successfully received one lot of information and now it's ready for the next. XMODEM is the commonest handshaking device (Xon/Xoff in the Set Serial Handshake dialog), though a few printers use Dsr/Dtr. Your best bet is to leave these at the default settings – both Xon/Xoff and Dsr/Dtr set to On – since this will work in the majority of cases.

If not, well, it's time to call in the experts, since setting up awkward printers can require more technical know-how than we've got space to explore here.

DATA SECURITY

Data security is something which companies the world over spend many millions of pounds on. Security guards, strong-boxes, password-protected computers, all designed to keep data away from prying eyes – those who shouldn't be seeing it. Even governments maintain James Bond-like security services and stringent laws in an effort to contain the poking about of their citizens. And that same data security is an issue for you too.

Not just because your personal details are held on computers all around the world, but because the data *you* hold on *others* is important and needs to be protected too. After all, you don't want a minion at work, marvelling at your Psion miniature computer, to open up the word processor and read a letter recommending his or her departure at the earliest convenience, do you? 'Could lead to some very dramatic moments...

It isn't just a problem of keeping away prying eyes either. All battery-operated computers are vulnerable to inadvertent losses of power. And if the batteries go down, so does the machine's RAM, taking your data with it!

That's why Psion provided your new machine with built-in data protection in the form of passwords to keep away petty

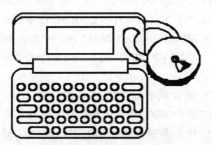

The Series 3 provides full data protection in the form of passwords, file locking and more...

spies, and battery back-up to prevent the possibility of lost data due to power failure.

Incantations...

The first thing you should realise about passwords is that a system protected by one is just as impenetrable to *you* as to anyone else.

• **If you assign a password to a document or to the Series 3 itself and then forget it, prying eyes won't be able to read it - and neither will you!**

To be really secure, passwords should be nonsensical words consisting of non-alphanumeric characters. By using words which can't be found in a dictionary and can't be directly associated with you (the name of your spouse, vehicle registration number and so on), the data stands a much better chance of remaining protected.

In addition, for comprehensive protection, multiple passwords should be used. If you assign only one password to both the system and a document, or to all the documents, and that word is guessed by an intruder, they'll have access to everything on the system.

Unfortunately, the best methods for ensuring complete protection also ensure a greater likelihood of your forgetting the passwords and being locked out of your own data. Several nonsensical words containing or consisting entirely of control characters are almost impossible to remember without being written down. And if you do that, how can you possibly be sure of their integrity?

By now, you're probably beginning to see how great the problems of data protection can be. The only certain thing is that no system is entirely safe from the unwanted attentions of intruders, and that sooner or later, you're going to forget a password.

But given that no system is completely safe, it *is* possible to render it impenetrable to all but the most ardent intruder.

Opportunist snoopers will rarely spend more than a few minutes attempting to crack your passwords, and the Series 3 has a big advantage in that it will probably be carried with you - in a shirt or skirt pocket for example - for most of its working life. Unlike desktop machines which sit around for hours vulnerable to attack from all quarters.

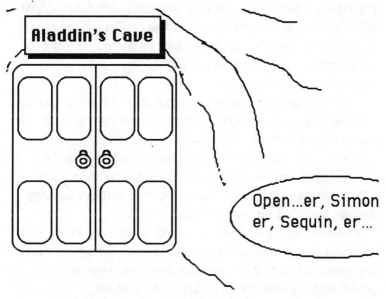

Forget the password, and the machine is as impenetrable to you as would-be intruders!

Choice protection

The Series 3 offers several choices for password protection.

• **The simplest password protection is choosing to protect the entire system, so that whenever the machine is switched on a password must be entered before it can be used.**

This is the best option if you have a lot of word processor and database files to protect and you don't want to assign individual passwords to each of them (which you might then forget).

To password-protect the system, summon the System menu bar (by pressing the System button then pressing the Menu key at the bottom left of the keyboard), select the Special menu using the cursor keys and choose Password. The Set Password dialog is displayed with a prompt for you to enter a password, confirm it, and switch password protection on. A cursor is placed at the beginning of the Enter a Password field - you've got to enter a password before it can be confirmed – so start typing. Passwords can consist of any character available from the keyboard, including tabs and the like, but you're limited to a maximum of eight characters.

As each character is entered, a padlock symbol is displayed and the cursor moves along the field to the right. The padlocks are to stop anyone from being able to read the password over your shoulder. Should you make a typing mistake, use the Delete key to remove the character to the left of the cursor.

• **You can leave the Set Password dialog without actually setting anything by pressing Esc.**

When you've entered the password, press Enter to move the cursor to the Confirm password line, and re-type the password. If you've made a mistake, you'll be informed of the fact and prompted to re-enter the original password again.

.Finally, press Enter to confirm the amended information, leave the dialog and switch password protection on. Now try this. Switch off the Series 3, wait a moment or two and switch back on.

You'll be presented with a message at the top of the screen telling you the system is password protected, and displaying the current time and date. There's also a prompt for you to enter the system password.

To use the computer, enter the password. The password dialog is case-insensitive - you can use upper or lower case characters or a mixture of both.

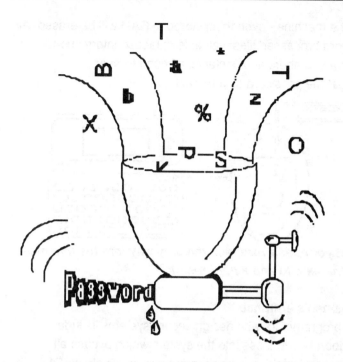

Include non-alphanumeric characters in your passwords, and don't worry about entering correct case – the Series 3 ignores case!

Meltdown!

Unless you've chosen a really obvious password such as your forename or address or something, the machine is now protected from all casual tampering. It will also be protected from you, should you forget the password. If the worst happens, and you do forget, the only way back into the system is via a hard reset – you simply can't use the machine unless you remember the password or do the reset.

A hard reset is achieved by holding down the On/Esc key and poking an unfurled paper clip or some such into the little hole above and slightly to the left of that key. This will completely reset the machine - everything stored in RAM will be erased. All your word processed files, valuable database information, telephone numbers and contacts, all gone forever.

Forget the password at your peril...

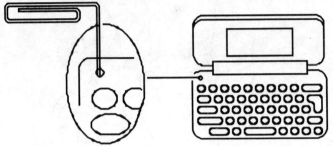

Forget your password, and the only way into the machine is via paper clip and a hard reset!

Tradesman's entrance

Many programmers who design secure systems include 'backdoors' - entrances into the system which bypass all security and which only the programmer knows about. Of course, there's no *documented* backdoor into the Series 3 - if it was documented, it wouldn't be a backdoor, would it? But we feel sure that there must be some way into a machine which refuses to respond to the wrong password. Don't, whatever you do, *rely* on the possibility however...

Turning password protection off

Summon the System menu bar, select Password from the Special menu (alternatively, press Psion-W) and enter the existing password into the Password Protected dialog (you'll be prompted if you inadvertently enter the password incorrectly). The Password Protected dialog disappears and the Change Password dialog is displayed in its place.

You'll see that the Password set field is currently highlighted. To switch the password off, use the left or right arrow keys. As you press on of these, the On/Off prompt in the field will toggle to the other state (i.e. if it's on, it will switch off and so on). Toggle the password off, then press Enter. The dialog disappears.

Now switch off the Series 3, wait a second or two, and switch back on. The machine is instantly available without you having to enter a password.

The password is still there, however. Try this. Press Psion-W to summon the Password dialog and, even though you've switched password protection off, you'll be prompted for the password before being allowed to access the password menu. Why? Because you might not want to password-protect the system, but that doesn't mean you want an intruder to access the password dialog and see what's written there...

In addition, anyone with access to the Change password dialog, has the power to password-protect the system. And that means someone might lock you out of your own computer!

Switch the password back on by reversing the procedure outlined above.

Password protection: a tip
Always set a system password. You don't have to have the password switched on – that is, you can switch it off so that access to the system is freely available, but by setting a password, you will automatically stop intruders from accessing the password dialog – they won't be able to learn the password or lock you out by changing it.

Changing the system password
Press Psion-W to summon the Change Password dialog. You'll be prompted for the existing password which you must enter before being allowed to proceed.

When the Change Password dialog is displayed, use the down-arrow key to move the cursor to the New Password field,

169

then enter the new password. Press Enter to move to the Conform password field and re-type the password. If all is well (i.e. if you confirm the password correctly), the dialog disappears and the password is changed.

Removing the system password

It's also possible to remove the system password altogether, so that you're not even prompted for it when summoning the password dialog. To do this, press Psion-W, enter the current password when prompted then, on Change Password dialog, use the down-arrow to move to New password and press Enter. Nothing else, just Enter. The cursor will move to the Confirm password field whereupon you press Enter again. The dialog is removed and the message 'Password not confirmed' is displayed. The system password is now completely removed.

File locking

As well as barring the system's front door, it's possible to lock up individual rooms. Perhaps you don't want to risk locking the entire system, but have a file or two that you'd quite like to remove to a slightly safer haven. In such cases, the Series 3 provides individual file protection.

That is, you enter the information you want to protect into the machine as a Word file, then use a password to protect it. Here's how to do it.

From within Word, summon the menu bar by pressing Menu, then select Password from the Special menu. Alternatively, Press Psion-W from within the word processor. The Set password dialog is displayed. Type the desired password into the Enter password field, press Enter, and re-type it into the Confirm password field. Press Enter again, and the password is set. When protecting Word files, there's no need to switch the password on – it is automatically switched on after you type in the password.

170

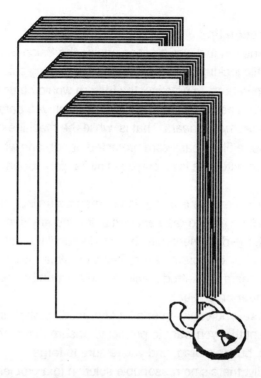

You can lock individual files as well as the Series 3 itself...

Once you've password-protected a file, it will be impossible to open it unless you type in the password when prompted. The system, and any other files you may have stored in the Series 3 remain unaffected.

One thing you must remember is that a protected file must be closed before attempting to use other Series 3 features and functions. If you leave a protected file by simply accessing another application, the file will be able to be read by anyone who presses the Word button.

Always close the file before using other applications, by

171

selecting Exit from Word's Special menu or by simply pressing Psion-X.

File protection tips

Although the manual which accompanies the Psion Series 3 suggests file locking as being useful for protecting a list of credit card PIN numbers, in practice, the feature would be useless for such a task. The protected file is always displayed *before the password prompt appears*. That is, while the machine is figuring out whether a file is password protected or not, and what to do if it is, the protected file is displayed in all its glory for anyone to see!

If the protected file is a long letter, then it's unlikely that an intruder will be able to read enough of it to do any damage (in any event, the document can't be scrolled until the password is entered so any off-screen text remains invisible). But with a list of PIN numbers, the intruder will see and remember all those which appear on screen!

Of course, you could enter a lot of preceding blank lines into a document that you want to protect to ensure that nothing is displayed, but its a drag, and you're sure to forget.

Basically, there's no reasonable solution to a problem that severely curtails the effectiveness of file protection. So be aware of the problem.

Changing and removing a file password

Summon the Set password dialog by pressing Psion-W from within the protected document (i.e when the document is displayed on screen, summon the dialog).

You'll be prompted for the existing password again and then the Set password dialog appears, either enter the new password into it, or simply press Enter twice to remove the existing password. The file is once again available to anyone who cares to look at it.

File attributes

Perhaps the simplest way of protecting a file is to change its attributes. These denote whether the file is read-only (i.e. information can't be written to into it) and non-deletable, hidden, a system file and so on.

To see what a file's attributes are currently set to, highlight it on the System screen and summon the Set file attributes dialog by selecting Attributes from the System menu bar's File menu (alternatively, highlight the file and press Psion-T).

Use the down-arrow key to highlight the Read only option, the the left- or right-arrow to toggle the feature on or off.

A file set to read only status cannot be changed or deleted (although it will be removed if you elect to format the disk on which it's stored). You can open and look at the file however.

The Read only attribute is a simple and effective way to casually protect files you don't want to delete.

Protecting data

The worst possible thing that can happen when computing is that you'll expend a lot of time and energy entering information into the machine and then lose it all by inadvertent deletion, losing battery power or some other 'natural' hazard. Unlike mechanical machines such as typewriters, which make a *hard* copy as they are used, data inside a computer is stored as electrical charges, and these are stupendously easy to wipe out!

Re-typing a long document, re-entering telephone number and address information and so on, is mind-destroyingly tedious and something to be avoided at all costs.

Psion realised that and are fully aware of the problems. That's why they've provided several measures in an attempt to save you from yourself (and your rechargeable batteries...).

Backing up

Everyone, or at least, everyone with a shred of nous, who uses a computer, regularly backs up the data stored on it. The process involves copying files and programs from a hard disk on a PC to a collection of floppies. If the hard disk crashes, the valuable software and information is backed up and can be retrieved from the floppies.

Sensible computer users spare no time or expense in performing back ups, preferring to carry out the task at least once a day.

And what's good for desktop PC owners is also good for you, too. The Series 3 is a robust machine offering a good battery life and a back-up battery just in case. But all batteries lose their power eventually, and the back-up battery is particularly easy to forget (even though the machine will prompt you when its power becomes low). Oh, and do bear in mind that although rechargeable 'nicad' batteries work perfectly well in the Psion, their power cuts out within a few seconds rather than slowly winding down like ordinary batteries - you can be computing one moment and staring at a blank screen the next!

Back-ups: SSDs

SSDs or Solid State Disks provide a really safe and convenient way to back up important data. These electronic equivalents of the floppy disk are available in two forms: RAM and Flash.

The former acts just like the internal disk built into your Series 3. Insert a RAM SSD into a drive slot at the side of the machine, and you can copy a file from the internal disk to the newly-installed SSD, but continue to use the file stored on the internal disk. If you accidentally change or delete it, you can retrieve the back-up copy from the SSD and only the changes you made since placing the copy on the SSD will be lost.

A RAM SSD is powered by the Series 3 batteries and also by its own internal back-up battery, so there's little chance of losing your data from such a device. Alternatively, files copied to a Flash SSD can be safely stored for up to ten years.

Backing up to an SSD

To back up a file to an SSD, simply open it within the application which created it and use the Save as option from the File menu, specifying the SSD drive when prompted.

Alternatively, highlight the file on the system screen and use the Copy file function from the File menu. After selecting the option, enter the correct drive (i.e. the one containing your SSD) into the To file: Disk field.

Back-ups: Other machines

The Series 3 is equipped with a serial port which can be used to connect it to other computers such as IBM-PCs, STs, Amigas, basically, anything with an RS232 serial port.

What this means, is that you can copy (or 'port') valuable data from the Series 3 to another machine and store it on that machine's hard or floppy disks.

This method is somewhat cumbersome when compared to using an SSD, but it does work, and the integrity of your data, especially when copied onto say, two separate floppy disks, is almost guaranteed.

• See the Connecting to a Desktop PC chapter elsewhere in this book for full instructions on how to back up and generally transfer data between your Series 3 and other computers.

And finally...

Be aware that even the most protected, backed-up data can become corrupted, destroyed by accident, or simply lost without trace without anything seeming to have gone wrong. The fault lies not with the Series 3 which is an excellent and able machine, but with computers in general. As a whole, they're delicate beasts and should be treated with care and, where important data is concerned, extreme caution!

TALK TO THE WORLD

Once upon a time, computers, especially *home* computers, were solitary beasts unable to communicate with other machines – owners were lucky if their machines could drive a printer, never mind transferring data, talking over telephone lines and the like.

Nowadays, if a computer can't communicate, it can't compute. At least, it's powers of computation are severely curtailed. Everyone wants to swap data and woe betide any machine which can't!

Fortunately for you, your Series 3, and Psion's sales figures, the pocket wonder is perfectly suited to compact

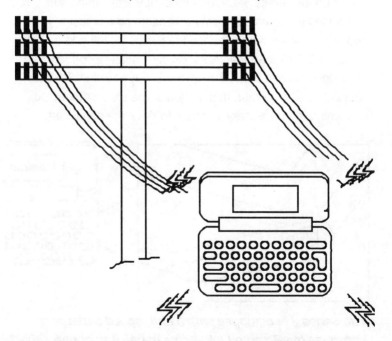

It's perfectly possible to connect your Series 3 to other computers via a modem and the telephone lines

communications. You can transfer text and data files to desktop computers for archival purposes, communicate over the telephone lines with a suitable modem, and generally interact with the big wide world.

It's all done with mirrors...

Communications is achieved via the Series 3's fast serial port and add-on RS232 cable (you didn't think you'd get away without spending even more money did you? Comms is a costly business...).

RS232 is the industry standard for computer-to-computer communications but unfortunately, the 25-way D-type connectors used for RS232 are far too big to include as a port option on the Series 3. Even the recent 9-way connectors introduced for comms by IBM and becoming increasingly popular are still too big – hence the Series 3-Link add-on cable.

Series 3-Link lead features a 6-way miniature connector at the Psion end and both 25-way and 9-way standard RS232 connectors at the other. In the middle, there's an oblong box containing the necessary software to drive the serial port.

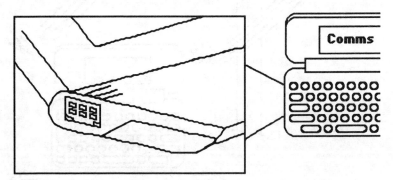

The Series 3 is equipped with a high speed serial port known as the Remote Link. You can use it to connect the 3-Link RS232 interface adaptor and then attach modems and high-speed serial printers.

Stupidly, the Series 3-Link is equipped with female connectors, and so are modems and standard null-modem leads (although, to be fair, many other computers are equipped with female connectors too. It's just that they don't already have leads hanging out at the back – the Series 3 needs another lead to connect to its RS232 lead in order to do anything useful...).

• **Mmodems are devices used to send computer talk over telephone lines. Null-modems are simple cables with the internal wires cross connected. This enables two computers sitting side by side to communicate.**

If you want to connect the Series 3 to a modem or a desktop computer, you'll need a patch cable with a female connector at one end and a male at the other (thereby converting Series 3-Link's female D-connector to a male...). Alternatively, it's possible to buy adaptors which perform the conversion. These are in the form of a small plug with a connector of either sex on each side. They're available from many electronics stores (Maplin's is the best in the UK).

You should be aware that we cannot go into the subject of computer communications with any depth here, there simply isn't the space. This chapter is merely to get you going with the Series 3-Link cable, and acts as a footnote to the documentation included with that device.

Feel free to plough ahead and experiment, however, you can't damage anything (except your credibility – you'll waste a lot of time and effort without proper guidance, comms is a tricky animal).

If you're not conversant with communications, get hold of a good book explaining the subject.

Wired for sound...
Plug the 'little' end of the 3-Link cable into your Series 3, and either the 25-way or 9-way D-type connector at the other end into a modem or desktop computer. Now switch on the Series 3.

179

From the System screen, summon the menu bar (by pressing the Menu key –but you know that now of course…), pull down the Special menu and select Remote Link or press Psion-L. The Remote link dialog is displayed.

You'll see that the Remote Link field is already highlighted, so use the arrow keys to toggle the link 'on' (the only other state is 'off'). As you do so, a baud rate will appear in the Baud rate field below. Again, use the arrow keys to select a suitable baud rate. Now press Enter to save the configuration and return to the System screen.

Press Menu again to summon the menu bar, and select Install Application or press Psion-I. The Install application dialog is displayed, and the first field, File: Name, highlighted. Down arrow to the Disk field and use the arrow keys to toggle C into the display (Series 3-Link pretends to be drive C).

As you do so, you'll notice 'Comms.app' appear in the File: Name field. This is the communications software contained within the 3-Link lead. Decide where you want Comms.app's icon to be displayed in the menu bar by toggling through the Position options in that field, then press Enter.

Comms

This is the icon installed into the menu bar after plugging in the Series 3-Link cable and installing its application.

Back on the System screen, you'll see that the menu bar now contains an extra icon with four associated files beneath it: Cix, Comms, Mci, Vax. These are script files – pre-written instruction sequences to enable automatic log-on to public access bulletin boards such as CIX.

And that's it. 3-Link is installed, you've switched on the Remote Link port and set a baud rate. All that remains is to connect to a modem or desktop computer.

Make the connection

Bearing in mind what we said about 3-Link having a connector of the 'wrong' sex for direct connection to a modem (you'll need an adaptor), plug the cable into a suitable modem, select one of the script files (say, CIX if you want to attach to that service, or else Comms if you want to connect to something else), and the software will do the rest. Now all you've got to do, is figure out how to keep up with the host's prompts typing on a miniature keyboard!

If you're connecting to a desktop machine in order to transfer data, you'll need a patch lead with cross-connections (a 'null modem'). Remember to set the desktop machine to 8n1 and the same baud rate, choose between XMODEM and YMODEM data transfer protocols on both computers, select the file to transfer and away you go.

WHAT'S GONE WRONG?

The Psion Series 3 is a friendly little beast. You select functions
as you want them from easy-to-follow menus, and you are
guided through every operation. But still sometimes the
unexpected happens. Here are some of these unexpected
events, and what to do about them...

The machine 'beeps' at you
• You've almost certainly tried to carry out an 'illegal'
instruction. For example typing text into a dialog when it expects
a number, or typing too long an Agenda entry. Read the
instructions again! The Series 3 is a very obliging machine, but
all computers are basically pedantic little devils.
• When the main batteries are on the way out, the Series 3
produces a small 'beep' once a minute to warn you.

An alarm doesn't go off
• Have you got the machine's sound switched off? Check the
Special menu on the System screen to check (Sound option).
• If it's been a while since you last used the machine, check to
see that the main batteries aren't exhausted.
• It sounds obvious, but check to make sure that you set the
alarm for the time and date you thought and not, by mistake,
some other one. If your machine is set up to display a 12-hour
clock, make sure you haven't set the alarm for p.m. rather than
a.m. or vice versa. If you're using a 24-hour clock, make sure
you haven't made a mistake 'translating' 12-hour times to 24-
hour times.

You get a 'Memory Full' message
The Series 3 has limited storage space in its internal memory.
While this is more than adequate for most uses, if you keep on

saving files the machine will eventually run out of memory. There are four things you can do:

• Go through your files, deleting those you don't need any more.

• 'Compress' your Data and Agenda files to free up wasted space.

• Buy an SSD ('Solid State Disk') to plug into your machine to store the information you're accumulating.

• Transfer less frequently-used files to a desktop computer for storage (via the appropriate Psion lead).

The display keeps going off

• The Series 3 will shut off the display automatically once the main battery power gets too low. If you leave the machine for a while you may get a few minutes' further use out of it, since most battery types recover after a short rest. You still need to replace the batteries as soon as possible, though.

• Check to see that the Auto Switch Off function (Special menu, System screen) isn't set to too short a delay. The machine may simply be conserving power.

The display won't appear when you switch on

• The most likely reason is that the main batteries are exhausted. As long as your back-up battery is OK, all your data is safe. You simply need to replace the batteries.

• Have you got the screen contrast set correctly? You or someone else may have altered it by mistake. Use the Psion + Contrast +/- keys to check.

The batteries keep going dead

Is the machine set up to switch itself off automatically? This is a power-saving feature which preserves battery power if the machine is left on. By default, the display is switched off after five minutes. This delay can be adjusted via the Auto Switch Off option on the Special menu on the System screen. Auto Switch Off can also be disabled entirely. Check to see that it hasn't been!

The Series 3 'crashes'
A wonderful term beloved of computer owners everywhere. It means your machine has, for some reason, become totally and irreversibly confused. Crashes occur when a computer is asked to do something completely outside its experience. If software is programmed correctly, built-in 'error-checking' will ensure this never happens – in theory. However, no programmer can predict everything a user might do...

You know your machine has crashed when:
• You get strange characters popping up on-screen.
• The display itself goes all... *funny.*
• All the keys stop working (the machine has 'locked-up').

The results vary. You might find that only one of the Series 3 applications is affected. You might find the whole machine is inoperative. In either case, the usual solution is a 'soft reset'. This effectively tells the machine to stop what it was doing and start again. All 'saved' files will be safe, but any work carried out on open documents since you last saved them will be lost.

• To carry out a soft reset, gently push the end of a paper clip into the reset hole just above the ON button. The machine will then restart itself.

If things are very bad, though (crashes really are unpredictable things), you may have to do a 'hard reset'. This is a nightmare scenario, since a hard rest tells the machine not only to stop what it's doing, but to forget everything it ever knew at the same time! A hard reset will leave your Series 3's memory as empty as the day you took it out of the box...

• To carry out a hard reset, hold down the ON key and *then,* push the paper clip into the reset hole.

Never carry out a hard reset before making every effort to

save your data. If only one of the Series 3's applications has crashed, you should still be able to copy files to an SSD via the System screen. With luck, you will only lose any changes made to the file you were working on when the machine crashed.

• **We know one very good way of crashing the Series 3. In Agenda, try carrying out a 'Repeat Item' on a 'To Do' note (these are note date-specific in the first place). Don't try this at home, folks...**

INDEX

Program To Get More From Your Series 3

First Steps in Programming the Psion Series 3
by Mike Shaw

With this book, anyone - with or without previous experience - will be able to tap into the incredible programming power built into the Psion Series 3 pocket computer, and so add to its range of facilities and functions. The reader is taken, step by step through the programming process and the 200+ word programming language, OPL, with the 'whys' and 'wherefores' explained where necessary.

The book covers the basic principles, the powerful graphics - including 'Windows, Menus and Dialog boxes' and the extensive file and database handling capabilities. It is profusely illustrated with programming examples that can be entered and run to demonstrate specific aspects of the language. A number of useful programs are also detailed, including a database 'shell' program that can be adapted to suit personal requirements.

Price £14.95   ISBN number 07457-0145-0.

Serious Programming on the Psion Series 3
by Bill Aitken

Starting with an introductory section, the book progresses to some fairly complex routines which the more experienced programmer will find useful. It discusses the internal structure of the "typical" computer, number systems and languages and structured programming, an area ignored by many programming books. This helps the uninitiated to design the code without worrying too much about syntax in the early stages.

The use of variables and the different types used by the Series 3 are described, all the OPL vocabulary words are covered, mostly by actually implementing them in routines. The author teaches the uses of loops, arrays, sorting and searching. In the area of files, the general concepts of data structures are discussed. The building of a simple spreadsheet is used to show the uses of the new random access file commands. The largest single chapter comes in the field of graphics. There are many commands to cover - more than 30. These are illustrated by progressively helping users to build up a complete graphics package which can be used to produce drawings for their own programs. Included as one of the routines is an icon generator. In addition to the graphics program, the user is shown how to produce graphs on the screen.

The book is rounded off by a comprehensive index, referencing words not to the page, but to the paragraph, making the index far more accurate. The book includes a large number of useful programs which the user will want to use time and time again. This is not only a teaching book, but also a reference work.

Price £14.95   ISBN 0-7457-0035-7